ADVANCE PRAISE FOR *The Art of Abundance*

"An operating guide for how to live a whole life."

—**John W. Lee, founder and former CEO
of Learning Curve International**

"*The Art of Abundance* is universally grounded and rooted in great truth. I loved every page! This is a must-read for a new era of financial leadership."

—**Leanne Jacobs, author of *Beautiful Money***

"The secret to a life worth living is found in our total emancipation from the fear of 'not enough,' and Dennis Merritt Jones succeeds brilliantly in awakening us to this truth."

—**Dr. Kenn Gordon, spiritual leader
at Centers for Spiritual Living**

"Dennis Merritt Jones is one of the canniest and most pragmatic figures in modern metaphysics. In this to-the-point guide he combines mystic idealism with workaday insights to help you think epically about the kind of life you want."

—**Mitch Horowitz, PEN award–winning author
of *One Simple Idea***

"Picking up where most other prosperity books leave off, author and spiritual teacher Dennis Merritt Jones offers us a deeper dive into understanding the principles and practices for creating a life truly worth living."

—**Wendy Craig-Purcell, CEO and senior minister at The Unity Center**

"Dennis Merritt Jones has not written another 'get rich quick' book. Instead, he has created a handbook for a life worth living, a mindfulness guide. With exercises to delve into, power points to personalize, parables, and beautiful writing, *The Art of Abundance* is one of those books I can imagine enjoying, again and again, finding gems with each re-reading."

—**Edward Viljoen, author of *Ordinary Goodness and The Power of Meditation***

"Dennis Merritt Jones walks us through the bumpy terrain of self-limiting boundaries into the self-empowered garden of material and spiritual freedom."

—**Barbara E. Fields, executive director of the Association for Global New Thought**

"Embrace and enact the ten foundational rules in *The Art of Abundance*. You will unleash dynamic growth and prosperity in your life."

—**Roger Teel, author of *This Life Is Joy***

The Art *of* Abundance

The Art of

Abundance

Ten Rules for a Prosperous Life

DENNIS MERRITT JONES

A TarcherPerigee Book

tarcherperigee

An imprint of Penguin Random House LLC
375 Hudson Street
New York, New York 10014

Minimum portions of this book originally appeared in different form in the following publications: *The Huffington Post* and *Science of Mind* magazine.

TarcherPerigee with tp colophon is a registered trademark of Penguin Random House LLC.

Most TarcherPerigee books are available at special quantity discounts for bulk purchase for sales promotions, premiums, fund-raising, and educational needs. Special books or book excerpts also can be created to fit specific needs. For details, write: SpecialMarkets@penguinrandomhouse.com.

Library of Congress Cataloging-in-Publication Data
Names: Jones, Dennis Merritt, author.
Title: The art of abundance : ten rules for a prosperous life /
   Dennis Merritt Jones.
Description: First Edition. | New York : TarcherPerigee, 2018. | Includes
   bibliographical references. | Identifiers: LCCN 2018001581 (print)
   | LCCN 2018002766 (ebook) | ISBN 9780399183942 (Ebook) |
   ISBN 9780399183935 (paperback)
Subjects: LCSH: Self-actualization (Psychology) | Happiness. | Success. |
   BISAC: BODY, MIND & SPIRIT / Inspiration & Personal Growth. |
   SELF-HELP / Personal Growth / Success. | SELF-HELP / Personal
   Growth / Happiness.
Classification: LCC BF637.S4 (ebook) | LCC BF637.S4 J666 2018 (print) |
   DDC 299/.93—dc23
LC record available at https://lccn.loc.gov/2018001581

Printed in the United States of America
1   3   5   7   9   10   8   6   4   2

Book design by Daniel Lagin

This book is dedicated to my parents, Russell and Evelyn Jones,
who, by example, demonstrated that a prosperous life is evidenced,
first and foremost, by an abundance of love.

CONTENTS

A Life Worth Living

Understanding the Art of Abundance
Changes the Rules of Engagement with Life

When I think about creating abundance, it's not about
creating a life of luxury for everybody on this planet;
it's about creating a life of possibility. It is about taking that which was scarce and making it abundant.

Health?

—Peter Diamandis

It is my sincere belief that the world doesn't need yet another self-help guru or prosperity book outlining the latest
techniques on how to win the lottery or how to go from rags
to riches in twenty-one days . . . or how to manifest the right
and perfect job, relationship, or parking space . . . or even
how to heal one's various physical ailments. What the world
needs is a new perspective regarding what gives meaning
and value to life; to recognize that *everyone* strives for

essentially the same thing. No, it isn't money or "stuff" on the material plane; it's something far less tangible and far more rewarding. Behind every thought, deed, and action of every human being of rational mind on this planet is the desire for freedom, inner peace, and a life worth living—a life that is filled with purpose and meaning, a life of fulfillment and wholeness. However, for the majority of the more than seven billion beings who share this planet, the idea that this type of life exists is impossible to conceive. Instead, they hold the erroneous belief that money—or material success—alone will garner the life they desire. This collective belief has been the cause of untold suffering for millennia. If you sit with this idea for a moment, you may discover there is a place within you where this same belief resides.

The point is to understand that beyond everything you think you want, what you truly seek is quite basic: a life of wholeness, a life of peaceful satisfaction. The irony is that such a world already exists—but only for those who have eyes to see it and faith to claim it. The problem has been that the majority of humankind doesn't know where to look for such a life. That is the purpose of this book: to help one open their eyes to the limitless amount of wholeness and abundance that lies waiting just beyond their current belief system. However, it is important to understand at the beginning of this journey that *The Art of Abundance* is *not* a book about prosperity; it's a guidebook to creating wholeness in every area of our lives. Creating a prosperous *life* is quite different from creating "prosperity." This is a book about creating a prosperous life—a life worth living—through accessing and utilizing a principle that is as old as the Universe itself: the Principle of Abundance.

Throughout this book it will be made clear that there is a distinct delineation between abundance and prosperity; they are more than two different words that many people take to mean the same thing. Robin Williams is quoted as saying, "No matter what people tell you, words and ideas can change the world." I invite you to embrace his words and open yourself to exploring new and different meanings for the words herein—you may discover new ideas that will modify your perception of the world and deepen your understanding and experience of what living an abundant life really means. My desire is that *The Art of Abundance*: *Ten Rules for a Prosperous Life* will speak to your mind *and* your heart. Not only do I want you to think about abundance and what it means to you, I also want you to experience how you feel about abundance. This is important because behind your feelings you'll discover your deepest beliefs lurking, often without your awareness, operating incognito. In other words, what you think about abundance may differ greatly from what you deeply believe about abundance and, thus, your ability to demonstrate abundance in your life. An exquisite balance between head and heart—thought and feeling—is required to access the principle of abundance that awaits your awareness and acceptance.

The word *rule* can be used as either a noun or a verb—and both are relevant in the context of this book. The thinking mind is objective and hungers for details. It is always looking for rules to follow; steps to take; a logical, linear process by which to arrive at a goal; the how-tos of getting there. It is for this reason that I offer, within each of the ten Abundance Rules, principles and practices that when followed faithfully will lay the foundation upon which a life worth living can be built. The phrase "practice makes perfect" makes sense; because the mind sometimes tends to wander when learning new things, the practices lay out a clear road map for the mind to follow. As a noun, a *rule* might be defined as a detailed or understood guideline, regulation, or principle that governs one's conduct within a particular activity. This is logical to the thinking mind, which operates linearly and deductively, but for the heart it is a different story.

The heart is intuitive and sees only the complete picture of an idea in its finished state; it doesn't resonate with—or even like—rules, it doesn't discern boundaries, and it certainly doesn't follow guidelines. The heart seeks a *direct experience* with any life-affirming notion; it does not require a

INTERESTING

me!

linear process by which to arrive at a conclusion because it sees only the bigger picture, an already completed idea. Because the heart is intuitive, it knows only the spontaneous, expansive joy, wholeness, and *freedom* that comes with the awareness that abundance is *already* yours by virtue of the fact you have been given the gift of life—and inherent within the gift is an abundance of whatever is needed to sustain you, to prosper you in every way. In other words, you don't have to earn abundance—you have to learn how to accept it, which is why keeping an open heart is imperative in the process of accessing the blessings and bounty of an abundant life.

yuk

As a verb, to *rule* means to control, direct, or exercise authority. Consider a king or queen who "rules" their kingdom with absolute confidence because they know they have immediate access to unlimited abundance. The intent of *The Art of Abundance* is to assist you in becoming your own authority—to lay claim to the good that is yours by divine inheritance. In this context each rule engenders a feeling of authentic power, which arises from *within*, experientially, when the principle of abundance is realized and actualized. Metaphorically speaking, you are royalty because you have been given sovereign control over the territory of your heart by the architect of all life. It is liberating to the heart and soul to know that you can rule over the domain of your own life— that you need not rely on the world for access to your personal abundance, fulfillment, and freedom. On the other hand, it is meaningful and reassuring to the linear thinking mind to have a clear set of rules to follow that will guide you and serve as a glide path—taking you the distance, manifesting in a life truly worth living; thus the "practices" that will be offered in each chapter. As you read the ten rules, you'll find your head and heart working in partnership to create a blessed life, the life you deserve and were born to have.

As a matter of "housekeeping," here's what to expect in this chapter and the ones to come: Chapter one is meant to lay the groundwork for the ten Abundance Rules, which begin with chapter two. The formatting of every chapter from this point forward is designed to facilitate a logical and sequential flow of ideas that make each specific rule easy to decipher and apply to your life. Each chapter is divided into five sections: **The Premise**, **The Problem**, **The Principle**, **The Practice**, and **The Payoff**. At the end of each chapter, there is a brief summary of takeaways for that chapter offered in **Power Points to Personalize**. At certain points throughout the book, I will suggest referring back to a chapter you have already read as a way to reinforce a point being made. Because each rule sets up the one to follow, it is recommended that you read the book sequentially and not jump around. Each Abundance Rule is meant to assist you in creating a greater flow of good in your life in ways you may have never considered, so it is my hope that you will take your time to truly absorb all ten and allow them to live in your mind and heart.

Let us begin with a parable about the abundance that awaits your discovery in the pages ahead.

All differences in this world are of degree, and not of kind, because oneness is the secret of everything.

—Swami Vivekananda

Once upon a time there lived a school of fish in the shallow, warm, clear waters of a secluded blue lagoon, protected from the crashing waves by a large coral reef. Every fish in the lagoon had been born there and most would die there, remaining separated from the vast sea, fearing to venture too far beyond the safety of the reef because of the legend of the lagoon—stories, passed down from one generation to the next, of those who followed the call of the mysterious Great Infinite Ocean and never returned. Many of the younger fish considered the stories to be a challenge—something to explore—because they considered the lagoon small and very boring. However, even they would admit that the mysteries and apparent dangers hidden in the unknown depths of the Great Infinite Ocean beyond the reef were intimidating. The legend made leaving the lagoon—which was convenient, comfortable, and safe—difficult to do. To better prepare themselves, the young fish devotedly attended school, making ready for the big day when they would graduate, knowing they would ultimately have to decide whether to follow the mysterious call of the deep or stay forever in the confining lagoon, living out their lives, swimming in the same circles, only dreaming of what life might be beyond the reef.

The day eventually came for their final exam. Being very wise, Master Mojarra, the head teacher, gave the fledgling class their assignment, saying, "Young ones, your graduation test is twofold: First, you must discover the secret to life. Contained within that secret you'll find a life of wholeness, a life of abundance, where you'll learn that there is more than enough of whatever you need, not just to survive but to thrive—and not just for yourself but for every other fish in the sea. Second, you must determine how you will use that which you discover to create a life of purpose and fulfillment—a life worth living. If you have the courage and faith to discover this secret, you shall transcend the confines of the lagoon forever and in that transcendence shall be found the greatest joy, a bliss beyond anything you have ever known. However, I must warn you, albeit right in front of your very eyes, the secret you seek is hidden extraordinarily well. To assist you I offer this ancient paradox in which the secret can easily be found: 'What you are looking for, you are looking with.' I must also inform you that you will not find the secret to life in the confines and safety of this comfortable lagoon, for it is hidden in the vast, boundless, deep, uncertain waters of the Great Infinite Ocean, a place where you have never ventured before. Now go, and when you have found the secret to life, return to me to share what you have discovered."

Acting as one body, all the young fish excitedly swam out past the reef and into the vast mysterious ocean for the first time, seemingly eager to find the ultimate secret to life, despite not knowing when, where, or how it would be discovered. Almost immediately, many of the fish began to feel very tentative about venturing outside of the known lagoon. The farther they swam away from the safety and comfort of the only home they had known, the more frightened they became; the terrifying legend of the lagoon lingered in the back of their little fish-minds. The Great Infinite Ocean seemed so big; it appeared to have no boundaries . . . no bottom . . . no beginning or end; it just went on forever. They began to tell one another, "The secret to life could be anywhere out there. . . . We'll never find it . . . *and* it is very scary out here all alone!" Finally, out of their collective fear of the unknown, they gave up their quest and, again, acting as one body, quickly turned and came scurrying back to the shallow, warm, and familiar lagoon they had always known—all but one fish, that is, whose name was Angel. For the rest of the young fish, the Great Infinite Ocean seemed so unlike the tiny lagoon in which they had been born and lived and would ultimately die, where everything was so seemingly safe—so well defined and confined—and where they remained, living the same life they had been born into, day in and day out. Angel, however, was different; she felt compelled to move forward. She knew she was being called by the mystery and depth of the Great Infinite Ocean, to follow her heart on a quest to discover the secret to life that Master Mojarra had so passionately talked about . . . and so on she swam, giving not a second thought to the frightening legend of the lagoon that had been passed down from generation to generation.

Back in the lagoon, as the months passed, the young fish wondered what had become of their friend Angel. Many believed she had fallen victim to the frightful stories they had heard so often. Then one day she triumphantly returned to the lagoon and reported directly to Master Mojarra. Angel appeared different from her friends. There was a soft, radiant glow of confidence about her, and she had grown significantly compared to her classmates. With a gentle smile on his wise face, already knowing the answer, the kindly Master Mojarra softly said, "And tell us, oh, brave one, what have you learned about the secret to life?" All the young fish gathered around and fell silent, anxiously awaiting the details of her discovery. Angel smiled and peacefully declared, "As I swam through the Great Infinite Ocean I continued to think about the paradox, 'What I am looking for I am looking with,' and I kept repeating it until it became my mantra. Then one day, while effortlessly drifting with the current, contemplating the immensity of the sea and the beauty surrounding me, I realized how comfortable I felt, as if I had been born in the current. It was then that I instantly knew the secret to life: it is my oneness with the Great Infinite Ocean; I was born imbued with its essence—I am swimming in it and so are all of you!" Barely containing herself, she said excitedly, "It's all about freedom! Along with realizing we are one with the Great Infinite Ocean comes the awareness that sets us free to be who we came here to be! Because we are one with the water that is present everywhere, we can use it to go anywhere, to do anything we desire—and the best part is, contained in the water is everything we need, not just to sustain ourselves but to thrive and grow . . . and there is *more* than enough for every fish in the sea!"

Angel went on to tell of the things she had learned and done, and the amazing places she had seen, all because she had discovered the secret to life: she knew that she was one with the source that provided for her every need, and that the lagoon, while a comfortable place to exist, could never offer the freedom found in her oneness with the expansive, limitless, open waters of the Great Infinite Ocean. Angel paused and smiled again contentedly, aware that she had accomplished something wonderful; she had achieved the first of Master Mojarra's two assignments. Now it was time to apply what she had learned, knowing that in the process, she would be guided to use her newly gained knowledge of her oneness with life to accomplish part two of Master Mojarra's final exam: to create a life of purpose and meaning—a life truly worth living. So, with peace and confidence, off she swam back into the vast unknown, going with the flow, fully realizing she was free . . . trusting and knowing anything would be possible if she just kept the faith in her oneness with the waters that sustained her and in the wisdom within that guided her to do what was hers to do. Meanwhile, back in the lagoon, those she had left behind were already busy spinning stories about how another one of their own had fallen victim to the legend of the lagoon by following the mysterious call of the deep. And there they remained. . . .

And so begins our journey.

CHAPTER TWO

Rule 1: Be One with Life

Connect with the Source of Your Abundance

The source is within you,
And this whole world is springing up from it.
The source is full,
And its waters are ever-flowing.
Do not grieve, drink your fill.
Don't think it will ever run dry, this endless ocean.

—Rumi

THE PREMISE

As the awareness of your oneness with the Universe deepens, you will begin to see through new eyes; everywhere you look you will find the principle of abundance operating.

The parable in chapter one is not just a story about a school of fish trying to break free of the confines of a limited life and too often failing; it is also our story. Like the majority of the fish in the lagoon, many of us have spent a good portion of our lives swimming in circles of sameness, in the shallows of life, afraid to venture out beyond the apparent safety of the "lagoon" of the known and to go beyond the metaphoric barrier reef, where everything seems nebulous, uncertain, and, yes, perhaps dangerous as well. The great barrier reef is a metaphor for our consciousness, which comprises the totality of all our conscious *and* unconscious beliefs, accumulated and warehoused in our mind from the day we were born to this moment in time.

The source of one's good is the Universe in which we live, an infinite well of "more than enough" that knows nothing about lack or limitation, where the potential for everything exists. The secret to life lies directly in front of us every moment of every day, but we fail to see it, perhaps because, like the fish in the water, we are so close to our source that we can't see we are swimming in abundance. It is the nature of the Universe to bestow upon all sentient forms of life an abundance of whatever is needed not just to survive, but to thrive. The secret to life is embedded in our DNA, but not everyone is aware; it hides in plain view, waiting for us to find it, crack its code, and bring our abundance into specific form. In the words of Ralph Waldo Emerson, "Man was born to be rich, or grow rich by use of his faculties, by the [conscious] union of thought with nature." Taking a bit of poetic license, I thought it was appropriate to add the word *conscious* to Emerson's quote because it is through the *conscious* use of our minds and the *conscious* union of our thought with nature (the Universe) that we can intentionally commingle with the source of our good.

THE PROBLEM

From time immemorial humankind has fought and struggled to survive. Throughout history the belief in "not enough" has dominated the minds and the behavior of the majority of human beings. It is the illusion that you are separate from the source of your abundance that gives birth to a belief in not enough. hum!

There is a lie that acts like a virus within the mind of humanity. And that lie is, There's not enough good to go around. There's lack and there's limitation and there's just not enough. The truth is that there's more than enough good to go around. There is more than enough creative ideas. There is more than enough power. There is more than enough love. There's more than enough joy. All of this begins to come through a mind that is aware of its own infinite nature. There is enough for everyone. If you believe it, if you can see it, if you act from it, it will show up for you. That's the truth.

—**Michael Bernard Beckwith**

While it is not really a secret, few of us fully actualize our oneness with the Universe in our lives because we have fallen victim to the "legend" of duality: the spoken and unspoken stories (beliefs) passed down from one generation to the next that draw their energy from one massive fear, the fear of not enough—not enough money, food, time, respect, love, land, oil, power. A variation on the theme is that one is not strong enough, rich enough, pretty enough, healthy enough . . . and perhaps the granddaddy of all not-enoughs: shame, as in, I am not *good* enough. This mistaken belief is fully inculcated in the collective unconscious of the human race. This is when the concept of duality—the belief in separation—plays out in an entirely different manner as well, dividing those who "have" from those who "have not." Irrespective of how you define duality, it has been the root cause of every war ever fought; it is the motivating force behind every act of selfishness, greed, corruption, and dishonesty. For this reason, understanding and dismantling the fear of "not enough" is a theme we shall mindfully revisit throughout all ten Abundance Rules because its systemic roots are buried deeply in the collective unconscious of humankind, as well as our individual minds. It is this belief that keeps us stuck in our metaphoric "safe" little lagoons, swimming around in safe little circles, believing we have to struggle to make ends meet in the material world, mistakenly looking to the world as the source of our good—to fill the "not enough" hole. The irony is, all the while, our true abundance awaits our discovery just beyond the known of our current belief system. In other words, we are consumed with the erroneous belief that our abundance comes from our jobs, the government, the economy, the lottery, our parents, our children, and so on. These are only conduits through which our good may flow, rather than the source itself—a limitless Universe. This lack of belief in a limitless Universe impels us to resist the natural urge to explore beyond the safety of the known; it causes us to contract and withdraw from the expansive impulse of life to a degree that it imprisons us. When this happens we stay stuck, possibly living unfulfilled lives, because we fear exploring the possibility that new beliefs can set us free to explore new horizons. Fear tends to do that; it drives an invisible wedge between us and our true source of abundance—and all the possibilities it offers—and thus between us and freedom.

To Transcend Fear, We Must Locate Its Point of Origin

All fear arises from a belief in death in one form or another—the loss of someone or something. It might be our physical death that we fear, but it could just as easily be the death of our bank account, job, lifestyle, relationship(s), health, reputation, and so on. Fear ultimately draws its life force from our belief in duality, a belief that we are separate and *apart from*, rather than one *with* and a part *of* the fundamental source of all life, all supply, all good: the Universe. Can you see this unbroken chain of beliefs working in your own life today? Our work is to reveal where that mistaken belief lies within us and rise above that sense of separation. As we transcend the collective consciousness that is ensconced in a belief that we are, or could ever be, separated from the true source of our good, abundance as a way of life will become natural to us. We will realize what true freedom really is and will be well on our way to creating a prosperous life, one that we know we are worthy of living.

THE PRINCIPLE

Prosperity of any type begins as the unformed substance of all possibility. With practice, living in alignment with the unseen principle of abundance will become as natural to us as is water to a fish.

Abundant living contains more than financial riches; we need beauty, health, peace and joy as part of living. From earliest times, man has been beset with supply problems . . . In the search for security he has overlooked the greatest channel for good, namely the self [his true Essence] as part of an infinite Creation [the Universe].

—Arthur G. Thomas

I am blessed to live in Florida on a waterway that opens to the Gulf of Mexico. Living on the water has afforded me many wonderful lessons relevant to the principle of abundance. What I have noticed is that on my waterway, all my neighbors' boats use the same water to float. The water does not support just certain "privileged" boats, such as the larger yachts. All watercraft, whatever their size—from kayaks to yachts—have equal rights and access to the same surface of water. Such is the principle of abundance. Because it is an omnipresent principle, it does not affect only certain people; it affects us all because it is equally available to us all, irrespective of the "size" of our vessel. Of course, the size of our vessel is another metaphor for the expanse of our consciousness, our individual belief system: the larger the boat (consciousness), the deeper it sits in the same water (source) with all the other boats; it just has access to more of the water based on its size. Using the Great Infinite Ocean as a metaphor for the Universe allows us to discover not just our place in it, but our oneness with an unlimited source equally available to every one of us. You were born into an ocean of abundance, and you really are swimming—or in this case, floating—in it.

How does this information make you feel? Does it bump up against any underlying beliefs that may limit the idea that you are one with the Universe, your source of all abundance? Are you at all caught up in judgment, influenced by what you may perceive in the world as scarcity—or not enough? It is important to begin to pay attention to those feelings, because beneath them are beliefs that need to be called out, challenged, and perhaps changed. Awakening to your true abundance is a process that involves mindfully exploring your deepest beliefs. Abundance is your birthright. The question is, where does this truth live in you? Do you sense that it is not only your right but your destiny to live an abundant life? Do you feel at home in your human skin? Do you feel a sense of being part of something larger than yourself and that there is purpose and reason for you being alive? As Max Ehrmann stated in his poem "Desiderata": "You are a child of the universe, no less than the trees and the stars; you have a right to be here." Again, try to remain in touch with the feeling nature of your being—it will tell you what is going on in the unseen realms of your deepest beliefs. This is the importance of emotional awareness.

Manifesting abundance is a choice offered to you every moment of every day based on the depth of your understanding of the first rule, "Be One with Life." While it is a metaphor, knowing and believing you were born in the "Great Infinite Ocean" of abundance is the core idea found in the first rule: remembering you are one with the source of your good. The hidden problem for the majority of us lies in the underlying belief that we are separate from the source of our good—that somehow we are destined to live a life of not enough. Perhaps that is because we have confused supply with substance.

Clarifying the Difference Between Abundance and Prosperity

There is a fundamental difference between abundance and prosperity. Each plays an equally crucial role in creating a fulfilling life, and it is important not to get one confused with the other. Abundance must precede Prosperity.

ABUNDANCE

We see the universe as a solid fact,
God sees it as liquid law.

—Ralph Waldo Emerson

Abundance is defined as "An extremely plentiful or over-sufficient quantity or supply; an overflowing fullness." Note that this definition does not specify form, only a degree that implies more than enough. This is because abundance is a principle that goes *beyond* form. It is a universal principle of more than enough of whatever one can conceive. Abundance is absolute potential available to whoever can actualize it by transforming pure potential into a solid reality.

PROSPERITY

Everything in our world, even a drop
of dew, is a microcosm of the universe.

—Ralph Waldo Emerson

Prosperity is "A successful, flourishing, or thriving condition."
In other words, prosperity is a condition, not a principle; it is
the effect, or manifestation, of abundance materializing in a
specific form (condition) and degree. The inclination of most
people is to think of prosperity as money or material posses-
sions, which it is in part; however, it is *far more* than that. We
can prosper in a multitude of other ways—an abundance of
talent, relationships, inner peace, good health, and the time
to enjoy them all.

As we deepen our sense of what prosperity is—and,
equally important, what it isn't—we shall see that irrespective of how we define it, with the proper understanding of
the relationship between abundance and prosperity, the portal to a whole new world of possibilities opens before us. Simply put, abundance is the causative principle of more than
enough, and prosperity is the exquisite effect. The question
is, which one do you tend to focus more fully on: the cause or
the effect? As we shall discover, we can't have one without

the other. The secret to life lies in knowing which one comes first and giving that our primary attention. The good news is, there is a practice you can introduce to your thinking mind that will assist you in focusing on the principle of abundance. Read on.

THE PRACTICE

> As a universal principle, abundance is omnipresent and therefore available to us every moment of the day; the challenge is that we are not always present and available to abundance.

> With mindfulness, you can establish yourself in the present in order to touch the wonders of life that are available in that moment.
>
> **—Thich Nhat Hanh**

From antiquity, the practice of mindfulness has been taught as the gateway to the present moment, including the principle of abundance. What is mindfulness? It is "remembering to remember" that the present moment is where the

secret to life is always waiting for us to show up so that it
may bestow upon us its opulence, often in the form of gifts
we seldom take time to consider as abundance. When I say
gifts I am referring not solely to material items but also to
the plethora of intangible good available to us without asking, such as our next breath or the next beat of our heart.
However, while we may not have to consciously cooperate
with the autonomic nervous system that keeps our heart
beating and gives us our next breath, we must be mindfully
available to receive life's plethora of other gifts. The Universe is continually giving us what we need not just to survive, but to thrive; this is the principle of abundance in
action. When we are mindfully present in the moment, we
are able to see the gift, embrace it, appreciate it, and use it
more fully. Mindfulness is a key player in recognizing, accessing, and activating the principle of abundance in whatever form it may be. *PAY ATTENTION*

Mindfulness Is a Cornerstone Practice in Creating a Prosperous Life

Mindfulness is the practice of calling the thinking mind back
to where the body is, wherein the two merge as one in the
present moment. Since there is nothing like a demonstration
to embody an idea, consider this mindfulness practice:

- Intentionally take a deep breath and *focus on that breath as you hold it*. Note that while your mind is focusing on holding that breath, your body is beginning to wonder what is happening; you have the attention of both your mind and body. Just for a moment reflect on how wonderful that breath is, and what a blessing it is to your body.

- Then, as you are releasing that breath, notice you are not fearfully holding on to it, thinking there is not enough air to take in the next breath. Your release is proof that, at some level, you must believe in the principle of abundance; you are demonstrating your faith that you are one with something that knows how to sustain you in *this* moment.

- Now take another breath, and while holding it in, realize the paradox that lies before you; notice that in *this moment*, your mind and your body are in the same place. Now ask yourself, Am I this mind or am I this body? Then realize one needs the other for you to exist. This awareness invites your mind and body to work as dedicated partners in manifesting a prosperous life.

- Finally, as you release that breath, consider the fact that, while your body can't be anyplace other than in the present moment, too often your mind is everywhere *but* the present moment, wandering in the wonder of the past or the future; wondering what may or may not happen five minutes, five days, or five years from now—or your mind may be dragging the dead corpse called the past behind you, reliving your regrets, resentments, or memories of the good old days.

• Now draw in one more breath, smile, and feel the joy and power found in practicing mindfulness as you release that breath. *Be Here Now!*

The Practice of a Lifetime: Making Mindfulness a Lifestyle

The point of this practice is that reliving the past or visiting the future in our mind is not necessarily a bad thing if it doesn't prohibit us from experiencing what can be available to us only in the present moment. With mindfulness we can practice emotional awareness by paying attention to our feelings in the present moment; they will reveal our deepest beliefs about abundance that may need to be identified and modified. With mindfulness we can challenge our BS (Belief System) and call out outdated beliefs that don't support us in creating a prosperous life.

Mindful living is a lifestyle—something that can be practiced anytime, anywhere—at home, at work, on the golf course, while driving or eating a meal. When approached with reverence, the practice of mindfulness becomes a way of walking a sacred earth, understanding that meaning and fulfillment in life isn't a commodity to be bought and paid for by demonstrating prosperity. Mindfulness creates a spacious opening that allows us to bring the gift of our whole selves to our world as well as to perceive the richness contained in the present moment and experience the amazing gift of life itself, the blessing of being *fully* alive. Henry David Thoreau summarized the importance of mindfulness exquisitely when he wrote, "You must live in the present, launch yourself on every wave, find your eternity in each moment. Fools stand on their island of opportunities and look toward another land. There is no other land; there is no other life but this." In short, there is no other place—there is no other time—where or when a life of abundance, purpose, joy, peace, authentic power, and meaning will be more available to you than it is in *this* moment. But the question is, do you believe it?

THE PAYOFF

Freedom! To mindfully actualize the principle of abundance opens the floodgates of prosperity. It is the belief in our oneness with "more than enough" that sets us free.

Freedom means you are unobstructed in living your life
as you choose. Anything less is a form of slavery. Yup

—**Wayne Dyer**

The ultimate payoff of mastering the first rule, "Be One
with Life," is freedom. Dr. Raymond Charles Barker defined
prosperity as "Having the ability to do what you want to do,
when you want to do it." Isn't that the ultimate goal of freedom? Notice that nowhere in this definition is there a mention of money or "stuff." Living a prosperous life means being
established in a belief that affirms there is more than enough
of *whatever* creates a sense of freedom in your life. While that
may mean an abundance of money, it could as easily mean an
abundance of time, or good health, or new friends, and so on;
freedom allows you to enjoy the life *you choose* to live. The
moment you transcend the belief that the material world is
the wellspring of your abundance, you set yourself free to explore beyond the confines of what holds the majority of human beings hostage to a life of limitation: fear of not enough.
By accessing the limitless abundance of a Universe that operates solely on a principle of more than enough, you release the
world from being responsible for your happiness and fulfillment. However, you must remember that—as the young fish
in the parable of the lagoon learned—accessing your highest

potential is only the first of two assignments. After you discover the secret to life—that you are one with the Universe—you must then learn how to "convert" that infinite potential into form, shaping the substance of the life you call your own, the life you were born to live. The question is, where do you begin such a trek? Angel the fish knew. The answer to this question awaits you in the following nine Abundance Rules. For now, let us just say the Great Infinite Ocean of abundance is calling you. Does it have your attention yet?

Power Points to Personalize

- **There is a difference between abundance and prosperity.** Abundance, as a universal principle, is unlimited potential—it is the *unseen essence* of more than enough of *anything*. Prosperity is the seen, outward demonstration of that which has been conceived. A sense of oneness with the principle of abundance will always precede a demonstration of true prosperity in any of its countless forms.

- **Fear of "not enough" arises from a belief in duality,** a belief that you are separate from the universal source of all supply. While it is virtually impossible to be separated from the wholeness of a Universe wherein everything is interconnected, it is possible to *believe* you are. You must be willing to transcend the collective belief (the stories passed down through many generations) that there is not enough for everyone, which always originates from a belief in duality.

- **The secret to life is that you are one with the Universe, the original and only source of all abundance;** you were born into the pure potential of abundance that already exists. To claim your abundance, you must be willing to leave the confines of your current comfort zone.

- **Practice mindfulness daily;** it summons your wandering mind back into alignment with your body, where, in the present moment, the principle of abundance awaits you. With mindfulness, you can become witness to your emotions, which may help reveal your deepest unconscious beliefs about abundance that may need to be identified, challenged, and changed.

- **What you are seeking isn't actually prosperity or even abundance;** what you really desire is the freedom prosperity represents and the inner peace abundance brings. The moment you transcend the belief that the material world is your source, you set yourself free to shape a new life—one in which abundance rules the day!

CHAPTER THREE

Rule 2: Be Aware You Live in an Expanding Universe

Observe the Impersonal Law of Expansion in Your Life and Learn How to Personalize It

The universe is a multidimensional creative process, constantly forming new facets of possibility for you and all living things. Expanding our awareness of the process, we allow ourselves to experience more of it. Every moment we can remember that ANYTHING is possible in a realm of endless possibility.

—Marianne Williamson

THE PREMISE

The Universe, eternally expanding at the speed of light, is perpetually pushing out, creating more of itself from within itself. The principle of abundance is the dynamic of this expansion in action; its mandate is to create impersonally through you at the level you are able to personalize this principle; your conscious awareness is that point of access.

In his inspiring book *Awareness*, the mystic Indian Jesuit priest and psychotherapist Anthony de Mello, S.J., tells the story of the disciple who said to his master, "Could you give me a word of wisdom? Could you tell me something that would guide me through my days?" It was the master's day of silence, so he picked up a pad and wrote, "Awareness." When the disciple saw it, he said, "This is too brief. Can you expand on it a bit?" So the master took back the pad and wrote, "Awareness, awareness, awareness." The disciple said, "Yes, but what does it mean?" The master took back the pad and wrote, "Awareness, awareness, awareness means—awareness."

DeMello's story points out that we tend to overcomplicate things and resist the simplicity of one of the greatest practices ever taught, one that brings us into alignment with not just the principle of abundance, but the deeper wisdom of life itself: *awareness*. The question is what are we to be aware of, and how do we facilitate that awareness? First, let us clarify that awareness and mindfulness are not the same thing. Mindfulness brings us to the present moment in which we realize our oneness with life, but awareness is the laser light that focuses on what is *happening* in that moment, and in the context of this chapter, what is happening is an infinite expansion of energy. Awareness in the present moment enables us to focus upon and experience firsthand the universal principle of abundance in action as the law of expansion, energy clothing itself in form—operating within us, through us, and all around us. Being fully aware that you exist in a living Universe expanding at or beyond the speed of light and are therefore a part of its creative process is a vital practice; it puts you in direct contact with the secret to life.

Debunking the Illusion of Scarcity

The present moment is where the principle of abundance lingers, awaiting your attention—or perhaps better said, awaiting your command. The practice of present-moment awareness invites you to mindfully see and feel the Universe expanding, pushing out, creating more of itself through you and all around you. The first step is to learn how to personalize *and direct* an impersonal principle whose only impulse is to expand—and present-moment awareness is where it begins. Mindfully understanding the equation that links you to the creative process starts here:

Infinite Energy = Matter + Expansion = Creation =
A Supply of More Than Enough

It followed from the special theory of relativity that mass and energy are both but different manifestations of the same thing—a somewhat unfamiliar conception for the average mind.

—**Albert Einstein**

Basic physics is defined as the branch of science concerned with the nature and properties of energy and matter and the relationships between them. In physics, the law of conservation of energy (not to be confused with the ecology of energy conservation) essentially affirms that energy is all there is; therefore, it cannot be created or destroyed but only converted or transformed from one form to another. What Einstein's famous theorem, $E = mc^2$, tells us is that energy and matter are fundamentally the same thing because they are inexorably connected and interchangeable; energy is continually transforming into matter and matter, likewise, is transforming into energy. The "c" in the equation represents the speed of light, which travels at 186,000 miles per second. Under any standard of measure, that means the creative process is happening faster than we can possibly imagine.

What does all this scientific data have to do with us and the principle of abundance? This is where being mindfully present in the moment with "awareness, awareness, awareness" comes in; we are energy converters. This is where the old adage "Thoughts become things" comes into play. In other words, everything is created twice: first within, in our minds, and then without, in our material lives. The intention of this chapter is to increase your awareness that we are conductors of energy—living, breathing conduits through which this creative process, the law of expansion, happens *every moment* of every day, and this can be either the good news or the "other" news, depending on the level of our awareness in the present moment. The more aware we are of this fact, the more we become conscious cocreators with an expanding Universe, directing the impartial energy behind all creation in beneficent ways that serve not only ourselves but our world as well. Remaining unaware makes us no less cocreators with the impartial energy of an expanding Universe—the only question is, are we creating an abundance of *more than enough* or an abundance of *not enough*? Either way, the

Universe is doing its job perfectly because it doesn't know the difference, nor does it care; it is hardwired to push out, expanding in and through whatever has a life force.

After discovering the secret to life—that we are one with an infinite Universe—becoming *conscious* participants in the present moment with this creative process is the next step; learning how to harness and consciously direct that energy is quintessential to manifesting a prosperous life, a life of abundance that spills over into all that we are and all that we do. Awareness in the present moment is the practice of a lifetime.

> You belong to the universe in which you live, you are one with the Creative Genius back of this vast array of cease-less motion, this original flow of life. You are as much a part of it as the sun, the earth and the air. There is something in you telling you this—like a voice echoing from some mountain top of inward vision, like a light whose origin no man has seen, like an impulse welling up from an invisible source.
>
> **—Ernest Holmes**

With enough belief in our oneness with what Ernest Holmes refers to as the "Creative Genius" (a.k.a. Life, Source,

Universe, etc.), one does not need to be a physicist to grasp the fact that unformed energy is all there is, eternally transforming itself into solid matter and, at some point, back into its unformed essence in an endless cycle. Ralph Waldo Emerson echoed the same truth when he wrote, "There are no fixtures in nature. The universe is fluid and volatile. Permanence is but a word of degrees." There is a message here for us all that we may want to be aware of: scarcity is an illusion.

We begin by understanding that because we exist as spirit, mind, *and* body, we are a microcosm within the great macrocosm called the Universe; thus the creative process that operates through the whole (the macrocosm) operates in the same manner though its parts (the microcosm). This means that with awareness we can become *conscious* cocreators with the unlimited potential of an infinite Universe. Understanding that the same intelligence operating universally at a nonlocal level also functions at a very local level—at the center and circumference of our being—is a life-changing insight. It is also the beginning of a beautiful relationship (and partnership) with an abundant Universe. So, take a deep breath, bring yourself into the present moment, smile, and embrace the fact that you really are one with the Creative Genius, this vast array of ceaseless motion, this original flow of life that is hardwired to help us populate our lives with more than enough of whatever we can conceive of within. "As within, so without" is more than a mere platitude; it's a universal truth. *Lot of responsibility Here.*

Everywhere we look we can see evidence that we live in an abundant Universe. We need not cast our eyes any further than the midnight sky or the vast resources of nature to see tangible proof that we live in a prolific Universe of more than enough. This is the law of expansion at work. To further elaborate, consider the following words written by Arthur Thomas in his book, *Abundance Is Your Right*:

The Sun could contain one million planets the size of our earth... Expansion of the known gives contact with stars that are large enough to hold five hundred million *Wow* Suns ... the average galaxy contains one hundred billion stars, while known space holds at least one hundred million galaxies. The galaxy to which our earth belongs comprises one hundred thousand million stars, with new stars forming... It is an expanding galaxy in an expanding universe which knows nothing about limitation or shortage. *A Bit intimidating, huh!*

With present-moment awareness we can easily see that we live in an exquisite galaxy floating in an expanding

Universe, which is eternally pushing out—creating new "star stuff" from within itself—and which has no boundaries or limitations and shows no evidence of slowing down. The obvious question we must ask ourselves is, why, then, we experience not enough. Why are so many people struggling just to "get by" when there is an eternal plethora of more than enough throughout the Universe? In other words, if we are truly one with this principle of universal abundance, why haven't more of us realized this and accessed our full potential? Perhaps when Albert Einstein declared that mass and energy are both different manifestations of the same thing, many of us just couldn't comprehend the full effect of what he was saying. Why? Could it be that we are not aware because we are preoccupied with appearances—the illusion of scarcity—and the apparent problems that seduce our minds into lingering in either the past or the future? When we are not present in the moment, it is impossible to access the pure potential—the unlimited principle of abundance—that lies within us. This is the intent of our second Abundance Rule; it is calling us to transcend "average mind" thinking by being so fully present and aware in the moment that we can embrace the known fact that the Universe is perpetually expanding and that we are part of that expansion. Remembering that what is true of the macrocosm must also be true of the microcosm is a daily practice that will pave the way to a prosperous life.

Potential Is Nothing Until It Is Realized, Actualized, and Utilized

> The truth is that we were born to have it all. And part of our handicap as adults is that we no longer understand our potential.
>
> —**Yehuda Berg**

wow

As pure energy, our potential is the one element to be found in all possibilities, omnipresent, and it awaits our command. In other words, our potential is unformed substance until we convert it into one form or another by shaping it with our deepest beliefs. Infinite potential has been referred to by some teachers as the cosmic glue—the connective tissue—that unifies the whole Universe. The entire landscape of our reality changes dramatically when we realize that we are immersed in pure potential; we were born into it, as a fish is born into water. In some eastern philosophies it is said that we are each born with seeds of infinite potential lying dormant within, waiting to be activated. Because the law of expansion has no bias, the seeds contained within hold *all* possibilities, good or otherwise; we nurture the seeds we wish to come to fruition. This, again, is why present-moment awareness plays such a vital role in what we grow in our garden of life; it gives us the ability to discern what the harvest will be.

As we shall soon discover, when we become aware of the pure potential that lies within, as a universal principle, we can begin to access that potential, bringing it into manifest form. A disciplined awareness coupled with conscious, creative, constructive, and life-affirming present-moment thinking will bring an abundant harvest of whatever is required to shape the life one desires. These thought seeds are worth nurturing in our mind. Consider the deep insight and implications found in this simple awareness: because the law of expansion is an impulse moving through all living things, we know the universe is conspiring for the infinitude of good that *already exists within us*, patiently waiting to be externalized, to be germinated, or perhaps more succinctly put, to be realized, actualized, and utilized. Now that we understand that we are swimming in an ocean of infinite potential, the obvious question is: What type of seeds shall we be energizing from this day forward because the Universe is listening?

THE PROBLEM

Too often the focus of our attention is misplaced, glued to what we believe is missing—which, in turn, directs the unbiased law of expansion to create an abundance of more of the same.

Both abundance and lack exist simultaneously in our lives, as parallel realities. It is always our conscious choice which secret garden we will tend . . . when we choose not to focus on what is missing from our lives but are grateful for the abundance that's present—love, health, family, friends, work, the joys of nature and personal pursuits that bring us pleasure—the wasteland of illusion falls away and we experience Heaven on earth.

—**Sarah Ban Breathnach**

From the moment we rise in the morning until the time our head hits the pillow at night, most of us conduct our lives on autopilot. The problem with autopilot living is that habit energy kicks in and we tend to go a bit unconscious, focusing on the struggle, on just getting by, on making it through another day. In the process, our volitional thinking mind pops into overdrive, obsessing over what we believe is missing rather than living with a keen eye and focusing on the law of expansion, which is manifesting within and all around us as abundance. As a result, we become cause to our own effect, ending up a victim of an undisciplined mind, and all the while, a lack of "awareness, awareness, awareness" is the culprit. In the words of Leonardo da Vinci, "Blinding ignorance does mislead us. O! Wretched mortals, open your eyes!" While the power of one's perspective will be more fully examined in the seventh Abundance Rule, Sarah Ban Breathnach and Leonardo da Vinci both lead us to the same conclusion: it is always a choice which secret garden we will tend, abundance or lack. Thus, the call to awareness, awareness, awareness must be heard.

Out of our own ignorance and a lack of present-moment awareness, we misuse the impartial law of expansion and end up creating an abundance of not enough. This is pointed out not to depress or distress you, but to bring you into full awareness of the second Rule of Abundance, which hopefully will de-stress and inspire you to refocus your attention on the possibilities available to you. The practice is to remember that energy *must* create form, and you are a conduit through which that happens. The law of expansion will have its way with you—of that you have no choice—but it is *completely* yours to determine in what manner that energy will serve you, what form it will take. An awareness of the fact that the law of expansion is always working in you and through you is vital, but so too is an understanding of how it operates.

THE PRINCIPLE

The Universe is in love with multiplicity, meaning that through the law of expansion there is a natural impulse to replicate, duplicate, and infinitely expand upon any given idea or premise that is firmly established in the proper growth medium.

The nature of the Universe loves nothing so much as to change the things that are and to make new things like them. For everything that exists is in a manner the seed of that which will be.

—Marcus Aurelius

There is no more exquisite example of the law of expansion in action and how it works than Mother Nature herself. As an experiment (in theory) to demonstrate this principle, consider the following:

Let us say that a large ear of corn has about eight hundred kernels and each cornstalk grows two ears. We can assume that one kernel of corn equals one seed, which will grow one cornstalk with two ears of corn, and that all seeds will be replanted for three generations, grow, and reproduce in kind. Most important, we shall begin by planting only *one* kernel in the soil, which is the receptive creative medium that is able to grow *any* kind of seed planted.

- **1st Generation:** Plant 1 kernel = 1 cornstalk with 1,600 new kernels of corn.
- **2nd Generation:** Plant 1,600 kernels = 1,600 cornstalks with 1,600 new kernels each = 2,560,000 kernels of corn.
- **3rd Generation:** Raise 2,560,000 cornstalks with 1,600 new kernels each = 4,096,000,000 kernels.

In summary, in only three generations, well over *four billion* new kernels (seeds) can be generated from a *single* kernel planted if it is established in the proper growing medium, meaning the impartial and receptive soil of Mother Earth, which will receive *any* seed planted and bring it to full fruition. This is the principle of abundance in action manifesting through the energetic impulse of the law of expansion. There is an intelligence at work within the seed (and the soil) that is greater than the seed, and it knows how to create more of

itself from within itself. It is also safe to say that if this intelligence lives in a seed of corn, it must also exist within every
living thing—including you. For the corn seed, the proper
growing medium is the field of soil; for each of us, the proper
growing medium is our mind, where our every thought seed
awaits germination. This is why it is vital to remember that
just as with the soil—which will impartially grow any seed
embedded in it, be it corn or a weed—our mind is receptive
and willing to grow any thought seed we nurture with our
intention and attention.

The practice of a lifetime is to live in harmony with the
impartial law of expansion, mindfully allowing it to serve us
in creating an abundance of whatever makes our lives purposeful, meaningful, and fruitful. Awareness that the law of
expansion exists is the only first step. Decisively putting that
awareness to work is what follows. As Ralph Waldo Emerson
wrote, "Once you make a decision, the universe conspires to
make it happen." The lingering question is, are you ready to
make a clear-minded decision to align with—and consciously
use—the principle of expansion today? The operative word in
the preceding sentence is *consciously.* "Awareness, awareness,
awareness" is the call to which we must respond in the present moment because it opens the portal to a state of mind that
aligns us with the universal impulse of the law of expansion in
a conscious, proactive, productive, and purposeful manner.

THE PRACTICE

Taking time on a regular basis to mindfully align with the law of expansion affirms that you are aware of the infinite possibilities inherent within and that they are fully available for you to use.

The more you lose yourself in something bigger than yourself, the more energy you will have.

—Norman Vincent Peale

Norman Vincent Peale's words are sage because, with present-moment awareness, they point you in the direction of unlimited abundance. With clear intention, losing yourself in something "bigger" than you can become a mindfulness practice that unites you with not only the law of expansion but also the limitless energy of life itself. When held clearly in your mind, there is nothing more potent than an idea whose time has come. Why? Because with present-moment awareness, we realize that an idea is a quantified unit of energy; pure potential, preparing to pour itself into a mold or form you are shaping in consciousness. While we shall expand upon this premise in the next chapter, trust in knowing you are an energy conductor, a director of pure potential. By losing yourself in an idea bigger than you are, you gain access to more of the energy that already exists within the closed system (meaning nothing can be added to or taken from the whole) called the Universe. This is the law of conservation of energy mentioned earlier, with which you can intentionally cocreate unlimited abundance. The question is, what do you consider bigger than yourself and what would losing yourself in something bigger than you look like? As a place to begin, consider that other than the Universe itself, there is nothing bigger than Mother Nature.

As a Mindfulness Exercise Consider the Following Practice

Daily, spend time outside and become the silent observer of the law of conservation of energy in action. Find a comfortable place to sit and breathe, mindfully bringing your focus to the present moment. Then, reflect on Einstein's theorem $E = mc^2$, and witness pure energy transforming into matter and, at some point, back into pure energy.

- Consider how water, as one form of energy, expands, converting to so many other forms of energy: Rain that falls from the sky converts to snow that converts to a stream that converts to a mighty river that flows through turbines in a dam—converting to electricity for our use—before flowing to the expansive ocean where, in turn, it evaporates and converts again to rain.

- Can you see yourself as an eyewitness to this amazing process? Understanding that it is all part of an eternal, expanding, contracting, and forever changing flow of energy with which you are one will build your confidence in the principle of abundance.

- While continuing to breathe deeply and mindfully, personalize the law of expansion and witness how it works flawlessly in your own life; note how you too are always converting energy from one form to another. One example might be how the food you ate for breakfast converted to the energy that powered your body all morning long, enabling you to go to work and exchange the energy of your labor for a paycheck that then converts to another form of energy called money, which, in turn, converts to yet another form of energy called groceries, the mortgage payment, the electric bill, and so on.

Repeat this mindfulness practice every day for a week and witness yourself beginning to feel at one with a Universe that is expanding exponentially in a manner that is using *you* as a conduit through which abundance flows.

THE PAYOFF

The Universe is continually conspiring for your good when you are available to consciously participate in the process. You live in an expanding Universe, which can only do for you what it can do through you.

Your greatest awakening comes, when you are aware about your infinite nature.

—Amit Ray

Logic tells us that if the unseen principle of abundance is available to one person on the planet (just as the unseen principle of gravity is), it must also be available to every person on the planet. As the architect of your own life, you have absolute discretion over how it is shaped. It's vital to remember that in its primary state, which is pure unformed energy, abundance is not something you can see, touch, taste, smell,

possess, gain, lose, own, buy, trade, or sell. Only as it is actualized in, through, and as your beliefs can the principle of
abundance be converted—or shaped—into a specific "form"
(or effect) that can be seen, touched, tasted, smelled, possessed, gained or lost, owned, bought, traded, or sold. That is
how much power you wield when you are consciously aware
of the role an expanding universe plays in you creating a
prosperous life.

As you make it a daily practice to visualize yourself merging with something much larger than yourself, you are an-
choring yourself firmly in the second Rule of Abundance.
Being established in the awareness that you are wonderfully
immersed in an infinite Universe—where the law of expansion is always operating—puts you on a fast track to manifesting abundance in every area of your life; as Walt Whitman
wrote, "I am larger, better than I thought; I did not know I
held so much goodness." As you begin to live consciously in
the present moment with "awareness, awareness, awareness," you'll discover that the Universe really is conspiring
for your good. The question is, how much good can you accept? The next chapter will reveal that answer.

wow

Power Points to Personalize

- **You live in an expanding Universe;** you are a microcosm within the macrocosm, and the same creative process that operates through the Universe operates though all its parts. Your awareness of this truth is your point of access to the principle of abundance.

- **The collective consciousness of humankind is mes-merized by the belief in not enough;** as a whole, human-kind lacks the awareness that we tend to function on habitual autopilot thinking, which has us generally thinking down, rather than up. "Not-enough-itis" blinds us to the secret to life that lies before us: our oneness with an abundant Universe.

- **The Universe is in love with multiplicity;** it is infinitely and impartially expanding upon a given assumption (be-lief), which your mind determines. What you assume to be true *becomes* your truth. The impartial law of expan-sion can increase only upon what your mind gives its at-tention to.

- **You are an energy conductor and converter,** a living, breathing conduit through which the principle of abun-dance flows and sublimates. Lose yourself in something bigger than yourself; work daily to train your mind to focus on how the principle of abundance operates in nature; align with that concept and witness it working in and through you.

- **The Universe is conspiring to assist you in creating a life of abundance;** through the law of energy, expansion, and supply, the gift of abundance is already available to you, and if you are aware and have eyes to see how the Universe operates, you can claim your birthright. Awareness, awareness, awareness is the rule of the day!

CHAPTER FOUR

Rule 3: Be Accountable for Your Consciousness

Understand the Crucial Role Your Belief System Plays in Creating a Prosperous Life

Consciousness is the fundamental thing in existence. It is the energy, the motion, the movement of consciousness that creates the Universe and all that is in it. The microcosm and the macrocosm are nothing but consciousness arranging itself.

—Sri Aurobindo

THE PREMISE

Your consciousness goes before you to announce your coming; it determines how you will shape your life, your destiny. Depending on your consciousness, you will create an abundance of more than enough or an abundance of not enough in every area of your life. When you become accountable for your consciousness, you become accountable for the life you create.

Once upon a time, a man seeking abundance and fortune traveled from town to town, never seeming to find a prosperous township that offered enough promise for him to remain there, and so on he would travel. One day, while walking to the next township, he approached a wise man who was just exiting the gates of the town the traveler was entering. The traveler stopped the wise man and said, "Kind sir, can you tell me about the town from which you have just come? What are the people who live here like? Are they prosperous? Is there abundance and wealth to be found here?" The wise man replied, "First, stranger, tell me: What were the people like in the last town you visited?" The traveler replied, "Oh, they were a greedy bunch of people who only looked out for themselves, never willing to share a morsel. It was not a prosperous town; the people were unwelcoming, suspicious, unkind, dishonest, and stingy; there was no prosperity or good fortune to be found anywhere. I shook the dust from my sandals quickly and would never go back." The wise man paused and then replied, "Ah . . . you best move on, then, because I have a hunch you will discover that the citizens of this town are very much the same."   *wow*

A short distance farther down the road, the wise man met another wayward traveler entering the township from the same direction, also seeking abundance and fortune. And the traveler asked the same question of the wise man: "Good sir, can you tell me about the town from which you have just come? What are the people who live here like? Is there abundance and wealth to be found here?" Again, the wise man replied, "First, stranger, tell me: What were the people like in the town you last visited?" The traveler replied, "Oh, they were the most generous people! Everywhere I went people welcomed me with open arms and offered me comfort in their homes and community; I felt a true generosity of spirit from everyone, and there certainly was no shortage of abundance there. Total strangers selflessly offered me opportunities to prosper in ways I could have never imagined! I would joyfully return and visit them again." The wise man paused and then replied, "Ah . . . then you should enter this township with gladness in your heart, my friend, because I believe you will discover that the citizens of this town are very much the same."

Over the years, this parable of the two travelers has been told with many variations. While the source of the original parable is unknown, I modified it here to serve the content of this chapter; its essential theme is timeless and makes the point very well: a life of not enough and a life of more than enough both originate from the same wellspring of our being, and the essence of either belief will follow us around like our shadow on a sunny day. How can this be so? In the aforementioned parable, how could two people enter the same township and experience two such different realities concerning abundance? What is it that determines one person's experience of abundance versus another person's experience when the external conditions are identical? As the old saying goes, we can run but we cannot hide—but hide from what? Ourselves! We cannot hide from our internal beliefs about the world and how it works; contained within the ancient admonition "As within, so without" is a dose of wisdom we cannot afford to ignore. Speaking in more contemporary terms—as reflected in the essence of the parable of the two travelers—your consciousness goes before you to announce your coming. This is why the third Rule of Abundance is so crucial. Consciousness is *everything*.

Wherever You Go, There You Are

Whatever we think, act, believe in, feel, visualize, vision, image, read, and talk about are going into the subjective state of our thought. Whatever goes into the subjective state of our thought tends to return again as some condition. So we, alone, control our destiny.

—**Ernest Holmes**, *The Science of Mind*

Do you recall the last time you traveled to another city or country? Regardless of where you went, along with your suitcase you took your consciousness. However, while you may have forgotten to pack your toothbrush or shoes, the one thing you can never leave behind, intentionally or unintentionally, is your consciousness. In the words of mindfulness teacher Jon Kabat-Zinn, "Wherever you go, there you are"; your consciousness is already packed and ready to go! The question is, do you know what's in your consciousness? This is an important question to sit with because the answer will determine your experience of abundance—as well as life overall—irrespective of where you go or what you are doing.

However, before you explore the contents of your consciousness, let us be clear what I mean by consciousness. Beyond the degree of your sense of being physically awake and aware of your surroundings at any given moment, there is another, deeper level to your consciousness much like an invisible suitcase that contains the sum of your beliefs, both conscious and unconscious. In other words, your consciousness is essentially bottomless and holds the imprint of every belief you have ever had, from the day you were born until this moment, that you accepted to be the truth about yourself and life as a whole. The good news is, once you recognize this truth, you can begin to consciously change your consciousness if it is not serving you in creating the life of abundance you desire.

THE PROBLEM

From the beginning, humankind has been immersed in a unified belief system that Carl Jung referred to as the collective unconscious, which is essentially the combined conscious and unconscious beliefs of every human being on the planet. At its core is a belief in lack.

One of the reasons it has seemed so difficult for a person to change his habits, his personality, or his way of life, has been that heretofore nearly all efforts at change have been directed to the circumference of the self, so to speak, rather than to the center.

—**Maxwell Maltz**

I once read a statement in *The Science of Mind* that in essence said the moment man, or humankind, stood upright and became self-aware, any further evolution ceased and all forward movement became his own responsibility, solely through the expansion of his consciousness. This statement would give one pause to consider just how far we as a species have evolved over the past thirty-five thousand years: We have put human beings on the moon and successfully sent probes to Mars. We have created machines and technologies that do much of what humans used to do—sometimes, even better. We have invented medicines that enhance the quality and length of life. It's really all quite amazing how "consciously" we have evolved . . . and then again, if we turn on one of those very inventions, the television, it may cause us to wonder if we have really come so far after all. At times, depending on what you watch, it appears as if we have gone totally unconscious, and even lost ground on the evolutionary path. Television and the internet are great means of seeing what lies in the awareness of our society. If these entertainment media are any gauge of our collective consciousness, to a large degree our culture seems to be thinking down more often than up. However, this is not a new phenomenon; it is an issue that certainly predates television and the internet, as evidenced by the English novelist Samuel Butler, born in 1835, who wrote, "It is our less conscious thoughts and our less conscious actions which mainly mold our lives and the lives of those who spring from us." Clearly, thinking down has loomed in the collective consciousness for a very long time.

As individuals, we are subject to the influence of the deeper collective unconscious, and if we are not mindfully aware, we can be easily pulled into its vortex. At the core of the collective consciousness lies a belief that there is a shortage of whatever we think is needed to create the life we have dreamed of, and we have unknowingly allowed that belief to spill over into our individual minds. The belief in scarcity— that there is not enough to go around—draws its life force from fear. This fear has mesmerized us and held individuals— not to mention entire cultures and countries—hostage in an invisible field of energy that has been passed down from one generation to the next for millennia. In the Scriptures, this fact is implied by the saying, "The sins of the father are visited upon [passed down to] the children." In other words, unless we are fully conscious, we tend to pass our beliefs about many things—including lack and limitation—on to our children, and they to their children, without even realizing what we are doing. That is how subtly our consciousness works, which is why we must become fully aware of and accountable for its content. This mistaken belief in "not enoughness" is inculcated in our species; it is the big green frog you must be willing to swallow first if you are to set yourself free to fully explore the secret to life. To put it bluntly, one of the primary things separating you from unlimited abundance is your consciousness, and only you can change that.

yup

In the 1960s, when the self-awareness movement began to gain some traction, *consciousness* became a buzzword. A whole new generation was trying to wrap their minds around what consciousness was, how it worked, and why it was relevant to their ultimate happiness and success. Defining what success "looked like" became an industry. Self-help seminars began to pop up everywhere, and the one topic that would get more people to attend than any other was prosperity. The "me" generation was ramping up, and the question "How much can I have and how can I get more?" was the topic at hand. Many people were ensconced in the belief that prosperity is about money and material things—henceforth to be known as "stuff." The logic that locked that belief in place was simple enough: stuff equated to success, and success equated to happiness; thus, the more stuff one possessed, the happier they would be. Unfortunately, it didn't always turn out that way. While some may have accumulated an abundance of stuff and increased their net worth, the question was whether their happiness quotient was commensurate with the material gain. Generally, the answer was likely no; the only thing that changed was the nature and degree of their problems. In other words, unless there is a fundamental shift in one's beliefs about self-worth and what constitutes abundance and prosperity, with more stuff only comes more problems. Today, still driven by a belief in not enough, countless human beings continue to pursue more. As long as we confuse *net worth* with *self-worth*, there will be a hole in the soul that no amount of stuff can fill.

> Prosperity . . . is consciousness. Prosperity is a way of living and thinking, and not just having money or things. Poverty is a way of living and thinking, and not just a lack of money.
>
> —**Eric Butterworth**

There is no doubt that given the choice between the two, most people would elect to be rich and unhappy over lacking and unhappy. Prosperity isn't about how much stuff you do or don't have; it's about a state of consciousness, and likewise, so is poverty. Clearly, the same can be said about happiness and unhappiness.

We know that another term for *consciousness* is our *belief system*. A belief system ensconced in a lack consciousness will do one of two things: (1) it will motivate people to strive and get more and more stuff, thinking the stuff will fill the "not enough" hole; or (2) it will cause some people to go in the opposite direction, even deeper into the hopelessness and despair of lack. After all, they have a demonstration of not enough right before their eyes—there is the proof, so it must be true! Sadly, their demonstration simply reinforces their belief in lack, and the roots of despair grow even more deeply into the fertile soil of a "not enough" consciousness. The cycle goes on and on, endlessly. In both cases, people are dealing with an effect, but if they were aware of the third Rule of Abundance, they could be dealing with the cause— their consciousness. It's ironic that the term *consciousness* is still widely used in the spirituality and self-help movement, and yet few of us ever take time on a regular basis to truly explore the depths of our consciousness and examine what lies therein, let alone consider how it got there. Why? Because we are often too busy, as Maxwell Maltz implies, obsessing over what we don't have, or trying to fix, heal, change, control, or manipulate the conditions (effects) of the circumference of our life rather than dealing with the cause that lies at the center: our consciousness.

We live in a Universe that operates largely on the law of cause and effect. This is why fad diets and weekend "success and prosperity" seminars don't generally work. While those attending may get some surface-level results, those results never last because people generally are not working at the root cause—where both our conscious and unconscious beliefs are warehoused—and this is where permanent change must begin. The same can be said regarding any other area of our life in which we might desire to see a lasting shift take place. Consciousness prevails. *Always.*

Getting to the Root of the Problem

> Until you make the unconscious conscious, it will direct your life and you will call it fate.
>
> —C. G. Jung

A majority of our beliefs are stored in the cellar of our unconscious mind. If we were to go beyond our thinking mind and dive deep into the unseen recesses of our consciousness, we would likely uncover many beliefs about ourselves lying there that are, well, lies; they are simply not true. The irony is, we tend to live from these beliefs as if they were true because we have never been aware of or willing enough to identify them clearly and to courageously question them, to call them out of the shadows and into the light, examine their validity, and challenge them. The belief in not enough will lie unnoticed in the collective unconscious of humankind—or our individual subconscious mind—until the conscious mind begins the process of self-inquiry and looks deep into itself. The image of an iceberg in the water is a classic example of how much of the mind operates below the field of our conscious awareness. It is estimated that the conscious mind constitutes 5 percent of our total mind awareness, meaning 95 percent lies below the field of our awareness. The saying "It's only the tip of the iceberg" perfectly encapsulates the conscious mind: the majority of our life is run by what lies below the surface—our unconscious mind, sometimes referred to as our subconscious mind.

As we mindfully explore the conscious and unconscious minds—which are two different aspects of one mind—we can identify errant and erroneous beliefs that do not support an abundance consciousness and begin to replace them with beliefs that do. Typically, beneath a belief that there is not enough lies the belief "I am not enough," originating from that hole in the soul known as shame. Filling the "I am not enough" hole can be done only from the inside out, beginning with a belief in our self-worth. Think about it: Can you imagine how worthy you must be to have been given the most precious gift of all, life itself? The only logical conclusion is that we are indeed *more* than enough to have been granted such an incalculable gift.

We Can't Change Something Overnight That Took Our Entire Lives to Build

As you read this chapter, continue to remind yourself that consciousness is the totality of your belief system—both your conscious beliefs and especially your unconscious beliefs that linger in your subconscious mind, below the surface of your mental, cognitive awareness. These are the deeply seeded beliefs—be they life-affirming and true, or less than life-affirming—that were planted in your subconscious mind during your most formative years. Eventually, those unconscious beliefs must come home to roost; they must surface and manifest in your outer world. As Sigmund Freud said, "The conscious mind may be a fountain playing in the sun and falling back into the great subterranean pool of subconscious from which it rises." Consider this: As a child, you had little or no control over the information (seeds) being planted in the garden of your ever so open, receptive, and fertile mind; however, as an adult, who is becoming more conscious every day, you have absolute control over what beliefs you will embrace and call your own.

It's important to remember that it took us however many years we've lived to build our current consciousness, and it cannot be changed in a matter of days. Instant gratification plays no role in lasting change; it requires time to reshape our consciousness. We build a *new* consciousness one thought, one belief at a time—by becoming the *conscious* observer of our thoughts (awareness, awareness, awareness) and feelings (which are only reflections of beliefs), challenging the beliefs that don't serve us in our wholeness, and then replacing them with ones that do. The practice reflects the mantra "As within, so without; as above, so below." We are always becoming cause to our own effect because our consciousness is how we access, personalize, and utilize the universal law of cause and effect. It is the mark of a wise person to remember that their deepest beliefs are "on call" every moment of every day of their lives. Consciousness *never* takes a vacation.

The good news is that we can manifest most of our desired changes on the outside if we are willing to first build a spiritual and mental prototype for it on the *inside*—again, one thought, one belief at a time. Furthermore, once this shift in consciousness begins, this new belief system has to be maintained like a living, breathing organism—we can't just build it and walk away from it as if we are taking a trip; we have to mindfully take it with us. A budding consciousness is like a maturing child or pet; it requires our constant attention to sustain its health and well-being.

THE PRINCIPLE

Your consciousness alone determines the degree of abundance that is yours to claim. With mindful awareness you can deduce where every condition (effect) originates first as a belief (cause). Only then, if you desire, can you challenge it and change it.

yeah

The law of correspondence works from belief to the thing... it is within our power to provide a greater mental equivalent through the unfolding of consciousness; and this growth from within will finally lead to freedom.

—Ernest Holmes

The "law of correspondence" in the preceding quote describes how the relationship between cause and effect works.

As you begin to form a "mental equivalent" of abundance in your mind, the Universe must respond to it in kind. The following is an excerpt from my book *The Art of Uncertainty: How to Live in the Mystery of Life and Love It*. Please use the visualization offered to build a mental prototype; it will assist you in expanding your consciousness, shaping it to embody a greater degree of abundance:

> The principle of universal abundance is composed of *unformed* energy or Infinite Potential until you *give form* to it by means of your consciousness. To illustrate this, visualize going to a well that is rich in resources beyond your dreams, and so deep that you can't even see the bottom. Imagine that this well contains whatever good you seek to be a healthy, happy, fulfilled, and whole person. Now, lower your bucket down deep into the well and, with no effort at all, pull it back up. How much "good" is contained in your bucket? The answer is obvious, isn't it? It all depends on the size of your bucket: A pint-sized bucket can hold only a pint of good, while a five-gallon bucket can hold only five gallons of good. But, what if your bucket were the size of a fifty-gallon drum . . . or the size of a swimming pool? How big is your container? Whatever its size may be, that's the amount of good you will have . . . and no more.

The concept of the bucket is a classic metaphor because it's one with which we can all identify. Think of your personal bucket as your consciousness. Your consciousness is shaped by your beliefs, and your beliefs determine the quality and quantity of what goes into the bucket. In other words, the bucket represents the level of your prosperity consciousness, which is based on your sense of self-worth as well as your understanding of the principle of abundance and your oneness with it. So, once again, the question is: What size is your bucket? If your experience in life isn't yielding enough of whatever you are seeking, don't go searching for another well, because there is only one well and it is infinitely deep. Instead, get a bigger bucket!

Building a mental equivalent of a larger bucket may seem difficult, if not impossible, if your current BS (belief system) has enveloped you in an experience of not enough. When Albert Einstein said, "No problem can be solved from the same level of consciousness that created it," he was articulating a paradoxical conundrum that you must understand before you can solve the problem. If you are always becoming cause to your own effect, how do you establish a new, bigger-bucket consciousness when you are stuck in the inertia, muck, and mire of a consciousness enmeshed in a sense of lack, that there is not enough? Do you recall the mantra "Awareness, awareness, awareness" shared in the second rule? In the context of this chapter, awareness lays the foundation for an abundance consciousness—but awareness of what? And how and when do you gain this awareness? We must gain awareness of our deepest beliefs, one thought at a time, and *always* in the present moment.

THE PRACTICE

When it comes to creating and sustaining an abundance consciousness, slow and steady wins the race. The practice is to start where you are and pace yourself. As previously stated, you can't change in one day what took a lifetime to create; but it is possible to change.

The key to growth is the introduction of higher dimensions of consciousness into our awareness.

—**Lao-tzu**

Do you pay attention to what you are putting (or allowing) into your mind on a daily basis? Do you believe you are worthy of unlimited abundance in every area of your life? Throughout this book, we will be exploring the quality and specific content of what goes *into* your consciousness, because where your attention goes, your consciousness flows. While this idea will be fully explored in the following chapter, for now, let us consider this chapter a cornerstone, a building block upon which a life worth living begins to take shape. Being cognizant of and accountable for the role your consciousness plays is crucial to your success. From this point forward, make the acronym ABC your mantra: **A**wareness **B**uilds **C**onsciousness. It is only through present-moment awareness that you can identify, challenge, and change your consciousness—one belief, one thought, one breath, one moment at a time. Study the following and see if you can discern the law of correspondence—the seamless cycle of cause and effect—at work:

Plant a belief, harvest thoughts;
Plant thoughts, harvest feelings;
Plant feelings, harvest words;
Plant words, harvest actions;
Plant actions, harvest habits;
Plant habits, harvest behavior;
Plant behavior, harvest character;
Plant character, harvest a destiny.

These "Words of Wisdom" (or variations of them) have been attributed to many people, including Lao-tzu, Gandhi, and Emerson, so while their source is uncertain, the words nonetheless offer a poetic and profound map, tracking the manner in which consciousness moves in a contiguous cycle of cause and effect, beginning with the pure energy of a belief (cause) and flowing to our ultimate destiny (effect). Simply put, a new destiny begins by introducing a new belief. This happens by backtracking from our current behavior all the way to the belief that gave birth to it. We effect change by mindfully observing our current behavior *in the present moment* and making a conscious choice to challenge it, and through self-inquiry uncover the belief that spawned that behavior. Then, if necessary, we introduce a new belief that inspires new behavior that supports our vision of what an authentic, joyful, rewarding, and prosperous life looks and feels like.

Is what you're
Doing working?

As a Mindfulness Exercise
Consider the Following Practice

The third Abundance Rule clearly shows that building an abundance consciousness requires great dedication; we must keep our consciousness healthy by maintaining it every day of the year. It requires great clarity, commitment, consistency, accountability, and follow-through. Consider the following points and allow your conscious mind to "marinate"

in them, knowing these ideas will seep into the deeper, unconscious mind, the storehouse from whence *your* truth
arises.

- Be willing to ask yourself—*and hear the answer to the
  question*: Does a belief in not enough live within me? If
  so, *am I willing to challenge that belief and reclaim the
  power I have knowingly or unknowingly given that belief?*
- Remember, transcending the gravitational pull of the
  collective belief in not enough is not a part-time job. It is
  a lifestyle—a new way of living.
- Your ability to observe, challenge, *and change* every lim-
  iting belief that has kept you from creating abundance in
  every area of your life lies within this practice.
- The key to maintaining this practice is to stay spiritually,
  emotionally, and mentally engaged in the present moment. Remember, awareness, awareness, awareness is required to reshape your consciousness and thus your life.

The consciousness you are building is a deep knowing, an
unshakable belief that you are one with a Universe expanding at the speed of light, continually creating more of itself
out of itself—and you are worthy of the best it has to offer.
Any belief that stands in the way of this truth must be

transcended. The question is, are you willing to do the work to go there? The next chapter will point the way.

THE PAYOFF

When you change your consciousness, everything changes for you. The world may not change, but how you perceive it—and yourself—will change. With that change comes a new relationship with an abundant Universe.

Consciousness operates in mysterious ways. One of those ways is that the old paradigm suddenly starts to die.

—Deepak Chopra

The reason the world is the way it is—and people are the way they are—essentially boils down to consciousness. Collectively and individually we are always becoming the cause to our own effect. The payoff that comes with becoming aware of—*and accountable for*—our consciousness is that it allows us to transcend the way the majority of the world thinks. When we are willing to make the investment of time and energy necessary to introduce new beliefs about ourselves, we enter into a different dimension, and life takes on an entirely new meaning. When this happens, the paradigm that continues to hold a majority of the planet's citizens hostage to an experience of not enough begins to wither and die for us personally and we are set free to explore the infinite depths contained within the secret to life: our oneness with an abundant Universe.

Power Points to Personalize

- **Your consciousness determines your destiny and how you see the world;** it holds the imprint of every belief (conscious and unconscious) that you have ever had from the day you were born until this moment. While other people may have played a role in shaping your consciousness, only you can change it.

- **The belief in scarcity—in not enough—has mesmerized us;** it has held us hostage, individually and collectively, in an invisible energy field of fear that has been passed down from one generation to the next, for millennia. The way to stop the "legend" of not enough from being passed to future generations is to become accountable for what lies in *your* consciousness.

- **Transcending a lack consciousness requires courage.**
  Self-inquiry is the practice that will open the portal to
  consciousness in a manner that allows you to effect deep
  change. You must be willing to ask yourself—*and hear the
  answer to the question*: Does a belief in not enough live
  within me, and if so, am I willing to challenge it and reclaim the power I have given it?

- **A new belief system has to be maintained like a living,
  breathing organism.** A budding consciousness is like a
  maturing child or pet: it requires our constant attention
  to sustain it. Practice mindfulness daily and nurture
  "right thinking." One way to maintain a healthy consciousness is to take time daily to read, meditate, attend
  classes, or in other ways "feed" your mind healthy thought
  food.

- **Instant gratification plays no role in lasting change.**
  It took however many years you've lived to build your
  current consciousness, so don't expect to reshape it in a
  matter of days, weeks, or even months. Building and maintaining an abundance consciousness is a lifetime practice, so take your time and stay with it. Remember, ABC:
  Awareness **B**uilds **C**onsciousness. You build a new consciousness one moment, one thought, one belief at a time.

CHAPTER FIVE

Rule 4: Be Focused

Consolidate and Direct Your Creative Energy
by Mastering the Power of Intention

Intention is the starting point of every dream. It is the
creative power that fulfills all of our needs, whether for
money, relationships, spiritual awakening, or love. Everything that happens in the universe begins with intention.

—**Deepak Chopra**

THE PREMISE

Your mind is the most powerful ally you could possibly have
in creating a life of abundance, purpose, and meaning—but
it needs direction. You are an energy director, and as such,
the more you focus your intentions, the more effectively you
can access and use the principle of abundance.

It has been said that the mind is a terrific servant but a terrible master. This is a worthy and timely admonition to remember as we venture forward. The preceding chapter established the importance of understanding that our consciousness is a manifesting tool that nonjudgmentally creates in our outer world what is *first* embodied within as a belief. In this chapter, we will deepen the awareness that our focused intention is a determining factor in manifesting a life of abundance. This is where repeating the mantra "Where my intention goes, my life flows" will be useful, because the mind-set to which we predominantly attune determines what goes into consciousness and becomes embedded. There is great wisdom in understanding and remembering that your life is shaped and solidified by whatever you focus upon.

MM

Our Mind Needs a Diligent Director to Set the Course and Steer Our Life Where We Wish to Go

Without *conscious* intention pointing the way, the mind, left to its own devices, may still create abundance, but not necessarily an abundance of what we desire. The operative word here is *conscious*. It is important to remember that the Universe doesn't judge the ideas and beliefs we embrace as our reality as good or bad, right or wrong; it simply agrees with us and acts upon them indiscriminately. The takeaway is that

if we are not mindful, we could end up with an abundance of
confusion, lack, and disappointment. Our mind *must* create—
it is hardwired to do so—however, our intention determines
what it creates. In his seminal book, *The Seat of the Soul*,
Gary Zukav clearly articulates this point: "Intention is the
quality of consciousness you bring to an action . . . When you
know your intention, you are in a position to choose the consequences that you will create for yourself." Suffice it to say,
knowing that we are one with our source—an eternally expanding Universe—is essentially meaningless unless we understand how to effectively collaborate with its impartial
creative process. The awareness that ultimately we must be
accountable for the content of our consciousness opens the
door for the conversation that awaits us in this chapter, and
on that door is inscribed the word *intention*. It is with our
focused intention that we harness our pure potential by consolidating and mindfully directing pure energy—the fundamental starting point and building block of all creation. Our
mind is a diligent servant, but it requires a conscious, focused, and intentional master—and this is our call to action.

THE PROBLEM

Often our minds are so easily distracted by the daily dramas and doings, the comings and goings of life that we sacrifice our ability to focus our creative energy solely on the secret to life that will set us free: our oneness with the Universe, and correspondingly, the principle of abundance.

Every action, thought, and feeling is motivated by an intention—and that intention is a cause that exists as one with an effect—If we participate in the cause it is not possible for us not to participate in the effect.

—**Gary Zukav**

We know we are always becoming cause to our own effect, which is why clarity of intention and commitment to staying focused on that intention is vital if we want to arrive at our destination: a life abundant with purpose and meaning. Consider the following visualization to illustrate this fact:

Imagine that your deepest intention is to take a road trip from Chicago to San Francisco. You and your traveling companion begin your trip with an animated conversation regarding which restaurants will have fresh, warm, locally made San Francisco sourdough bread, and you share your mutual excitement about riding the cable cars down the famed Market Street while watching the sunset over the misty bay. You have made your nightly reservations at motels along the route as well as at a lovely bed-and-breakfast with a view of the Golden Gate Bridge in San Francisco. You have your spending money, your car has new tires and a full tank of gas . . . and now you are on the open road; the convertible top is down and you are enjoying the many sights along the way while your favorite music thumps out a commanding backbeat rhythm that compels you to sing along! As the wind blows through your hair, you smile knowing you are well on your way to the city by the bay! Hours pass by, and as you drive through Nashville, you and your friend are joyfully jabbering away, talking about what a great time you are going to have once you arrive in San Francisco. You are so excited about being there that you decide not to stop to take pictures when you pass through New Orleans later.

Then, suddenly you realize . . . Nashville . . . New Orleans . . . ? You never *intended* to go to Nashville. It's not even on the way to San Francisco! "Where did I go wrong?" you mumble to yourself. "How did I end up in

PLAN?
GOAL?

Nashville? And New Orleans is nowhere near California."
The problem arose when you forgot to *pay attention to
your intention*, which took you in a direction you never
really wanted to go; yet there you are. In short, you took
your attention off the road signs right in front of you.

DISTRACTED

If this visualization sounds like a metaphor for our lives,
that's because it is. At the end of our journey on this planet,
many of us will find ourselves living a less than fully abundant life because our focus drifted from the destination (goal)
to the distractions—the drama and comings and goings found
along the way. Perhaps the moral of the story is to focus on doing fewer things and to do them more mindfully, and thus more
efficiently. The power, creativity, and productivity of a focused mind is beyond measure. The problem is, an unfocused
mind is equally powerful. If we are not paying careful attention to our intention, our mind can become our master rather
than our servant, taking us on a wild goose chase to places
we don't really want to go. While it is equally powerful and
creative, an unfocused mind is not nearly as effective in creating a life worth living because its energy is being defused.
An unfocused mind is a scattered mind, diluting its creative
energy by sending it in multiple directions at the same time.
To put this into perspective, think of a clearly focused mind
as a laser light concentrated on a very specific target. That

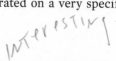

INTERESTING

target could be many miles away, but the laser will reach it because it is consolidating 100 percent of its power into a narrow, intense, singular beam. Now think of an unfocused mind as an incandescent lightbulb, emitting light in every direction but for the distance of only a few feet. The reason why many of us are not more effective in creating an abundance consciousness is that our minds are like the incandescent light; we are not focusing our energy on a specific target. In this case, the "target" is the principle of abundance and how it is applicable in our lives in a multitude of ways.

The Present Moment Is Where a New Cause for a New Effect First Originates

Our minds are scattered because we lack the focus and mindfulness to be fully present in the moment, which is our only true point of power. It has been said that everything is created twice—first in mind and then in form. The point being, the present moment is where all creation happens—first within as a belief (cause), and then without in the manifest world (effect). Having clear intention energized by an ebullience for life will shape and determine what that creation shall be. The key, however, is not to allow our passion in the moment to pull us off course from the fulfillment of our intention. *Focus* is the word of the day!

The road trip visualization describes how many of us live our lives: with good intentions but also with a lack of the follow-through that can be sustained only with our engaged attention in the moment. In other words, to achieve a specific outcome in life, our good intention alone is not enough to get us to our destination. We must couple *paying attention* with our intention. This, then, is how we set our point of focus—our metaphoric laser beam—and hold it on the target called abundance. Your mind wields awesome power. The quintessential question is, will it be your master or servant? The choice is yours to make.

THE PRINCIPLE

recipe for life

(Intention + Attention) x Belief = Manifestation. Energy follows the path of least resistance. What you train your mind to obediently focus upon establishes that path. This is the extremely impartial law of attraction in action.

Whatever you put attention on will start manifesting in your life. Intention, attention, manifestation; that is how the universe works.

—**Sri Sri Ravi Shankar**

This quote by Sri Sri Ravi Shankar summarizes how the discipline of a focused mind moves energy from cause to effect; however, the one ingredient he failed to mention is belief—but belief in what? While some may see this as a call to a belief in a higher power, it can just as easily be thought of as believing in Mother Nature or the practice of earth science. Irrespective of what we may call it, there is an organizing intelligence that permeates each living thing, which compels it to grow, push out, evolve, unfold itself, and uniquely express the essence of life that flows through that thing.

As we learned in the second Abundance Rule, we are one with a Universe that is expanding at the speed of light. This organizing intelligence—call it what you may—is already on the job, doing the heavy lifting 24-7, and it has been since the beginning of time. Our work is to realize that we are each a living thing and trust that this compelling power knows how to grow the results of our greatest intention through us. Herein lies the proof that abundance is not something we must create. We must, however, align with its omnipresent principle, plant ourselves in the creative soil of a receptive, focused mind, and be open to its flow. In other words, we have to be clear on our intention and attentively, with faith, hold our focus on the target, regardless of how far from our current reality it may appear, and allow the principle of abundance to do its part by finding fulfillment through us. As an example of how your faith in an unseen principle can be deepened, consider the following visualization:

> Imagine you love tulips so much that it becomes your intention to plant a garden full of tulip bulbs in the late autumn, knowing that by spring you will be enjoying their beauty and the joy they bring to your life. What kind of attention would be required to enable the tulips to grow and flourish? First, it would mean making sure you have selected the proper bulbs. Are they the right variety that will thrive in the growing conditions of your garden? Mindfully choosing what you plant in this garden is essential, but *where* you plant them is equally important. Are they planted in soil where they will receive the necessary amounts of nutrients and sunlight? Also, remember, they will require proper watering and feeding, as well as pulling and removing any encroaching weeds. Can you see yourself in your garden doing the required maintenance? With this amount of focused *attention* on your *intention*, and an ample amount of *belief* in the unseen principle of life and energy pushing out, expanding toward the light, you can expect to see a plethora of tulips—an abundance of beautiful flowers—in the spring.

In the preceding visualization, notice that you didn't once go to the garden *after* the bulbs were planted and dig them up to see why the sprouts had not yet broken through the soil. Instead, you had faith—you tended to your garden and trusted the process. You trusted that your intention, followed by the appropriate attention, would yield beautiful results: a garden full of tulips. You chose the correct bulbs (thought seeds) and planted them with clear intention in your garden (a receptive mind), and then attended to them mindfully, leaving the rest to nature. This is how the principle of abundance operates through the fertile field of your deepest intentions. When your attention is focused on tending to the garden of your mind, where your intentions are planted, growth is certain to happen. You hold the vision of your intentions by watering them with your daily attention, feeding them regularly with energy, confidence, and an abiding belief in something larger than yourself—the Universe—while at the same time pulling the ever-persistent weeds of instant gratification, diversion, distraction, negative thinking, self-doubt, worry, and fear. The result—a life filled with purpose and meaning—is a beautiful life truly worth living.

The Law of Attraction: The Double-Edged Sword

The vast majority of people are born, grow up, struggle, and go through life in misery and failure, not realizing that it would be just as easy to switch over [change their mind] and get exactly what they want out of life, not recognizing that the mind attracts the thing it dwells upon.

—**Napoleon Hill**

The term *law of attraction* first appeared in print in 1887 in a book written by the Russian cofounder of the Theosophical Society, Helena Blavatsky, but the principle that undergirds the concept has been spoken about for thousands of years. The idea that there is great power to be found in a focused mind backed by unshakable belief is not new. Buddha elucidated this point in the following excerpt from the Dhammapada, written well over two thousand years ago:

We are what we think.
All that we are arises with our thoughts.
With our thoughts we make the world.
Speak or act with an impure mind
And trouble will follow you
As the wheel follows the ox that draws the cart.

We are what we think.
All that we are arises with our thoughts.
With our thoughts we make the world.

Speak or act with a pure mind
And happiness will follow you
As your shadow, unshakable.

Please note that the Buddha's admonition is announcing both the good news and the "other news" about the law of attraction: it plays no favorites; like a universal magnet, it draws to us that which is most predominant in our mind. People wonder why they continue to re-create the same challenges over and over again, and all the while, it is the law of attraction doing what it does best—giving us what we primarily focus our attention on. This is why mindfulness is so important; it allows us to eavesdrop on what is percolating in our minds and hold a mental housecleaning party if necessary. As you'll see in the following excerpt from my book *Your (Re)Defining Moments: Becoming Who You Were Born to Be*, there is no area of our lives in which the law of attraction isn't on duty 24-7:

The law of attraction will never fail in drawing to us whatever reflects our predominant thoughts and deepest beliefs. As an example, many of us have gone from one disastrous relationship or unsatisfactory job to the next, and then the next, ad infinitum, never stopping long enough to explore the possibility that each failed experience had something to teach us. You can run but you can't hide from yourself. While the next person's name and hair color may change, the "issues" don't. While the next job may appear to have different coworkers, amazingly enough, the same "problem" people show up in different bodies. We can't outrun our self-limiting behaviors and beliefs because they will follow us like our own shadow; however, we can transcend them by exposing them to the light of present-moment awareness. The practice is to pay attention to what is going on in the moment and learn what it has to teach us.

Knowing that the principle of abundance applies to every area of your life, where might you be using the law of attraction unknowingly in a less than beneficial manner? This is why the fourth Rule of Abundance, "Be Focused," plays such an important role in creating the life you desire.

THE PRACTICE

Because the belief in not enough is inculcated in the collective unconscious, training your mind to focus on the principle of abundance—that there is enough for everyone—and keeping it there is the practice of a lifetime.

That which thought has done, thought can undo. Lifelong
habits of wrong thinking can be consciously and deliber-
ately neutralized, and an entirely new order of mental
and emotional reaction established in mind. Merely to
abstain from wrong thinking is not enough; there must
be active right thinking.

—**Ernest Holmes**

The conscious mind is essentially "monophonic," meaning it can think only one thought at a time. That is great news
because it makes learning how to focus your attention on
your intention much easier. Most of us have heard the phrase
"Garbage in, garbage out" (GIGO) and understand what it
means. With awareness you can begin to consciously monitor what you are thinking and identify thoughts and beliefs
that no longer serve you—but that is not enough! After identifying your wrong thinking, as Holmes points out, you must
insert right thinking in its place. While you can't "unthink"
a thought, you can mindfully identify and "undo" a thought
by choosing a new thought that neutralizes it; in this case,
one based on a belief that because you are one with your
source, you are worthy of the best life has to offer.

This process is how you build an abundance consciousness, and it begins with your next thought. The practice is to

be present enough in the moment to mindfully witness where your mind wants to go and then, as Don Miguel Ruiz, author of *The Four Agreements*, says, "stalk your thoughts," catching the ones that are not affirming your worthiness—your oneness with life—at which point you can challenge the thoughts and change them, one at a time. This is the power of focusing your attention on your intention, irrespective of where you are or what you are doing.

Practice 1

BECOME A CONSCIOUS OBSERVER OF YOURSELF IN ACTION.

In his classic book, *The Science of Mind*, Ernest Holmes points out the inevitable relationship between our focused point of attention and our ultimate destiny: "Whatever we think, act, believe in, feel, visualize, vision, image, read, and talk about are going into the subjective state of our thought. Whatever goes into the subjective state of our thought tends to return again as some condition. So we, alone, control our destiny." Holmes's words set the stage for the following self-inquiry practice. With clear intention you can train your mind to focus on the principle of abundance in the present moment. Note that paying attention to your intention can go far beyond manifesting material abundance.

1. The next time you turn on the television, watch a movie, or start to read an article or a book, be aware of the intent of what you are watching or reading, realizing that the essence of its content is seeping ever so inconspicuously into your consciousness (remember ABC).

   SELF-INQUIRY: Ask yourself, Do the words I read or the programs I watch align my mind with the principle of abundance? Do they feed my mind with healthy, life-affirming images, constructive ideas and story lines, or is the content less than soul nourishing?

2. Become aware of your relationships—both intimate and casual—because they each reflect some aspect of your current consciousness. Remember, the Universe is listening, and it takes what you affirm for yourself seriously. The type of relationships you have speaks volumes as to who you think you are and how worthy you believe you are.

   SELF-INQUIRY: Ask yourself, Are my relationships with people who inspire and lift me to higher levels of thinking? Or do our conversations revolve around a belief in not enough or gossip or complaining about how "bad" things are—essentially staring at what's wrong with life rather than what's right?

3. The next time you are in a restaurant, as you begin looking at the menu, notice where your attention goes first.

This practice will allow you to see your unconscious intentions about the relationship you have with yourself and with the principle of abundance.

SELF-INQUIRY: Do my eyes first drift to the side where the food items are listed, or to the side where the prices are listed? Is my choice of meal determined by its price or by how much the meal actually appeals to me?

4. Are you a coupon clipper? Let us be clear: seeking to save money is not a bad thing, but understanding your motivation behind it can reveal your current state of abundance consciousness. When shopping or spending money on yourself, where does your attention go initially? Do you find yourself looking *first* for sale items and special bargains? Self-worth can also determine your spending habits. This is not to say you should spend foolishly or not be prudent enough to take advantage of a great deal that pops up when shopping. The point of this practice is to witness your current abundance consciousness as well as how much value you place on yourself.

SELF-INQUIRY: What is my motivation behind bargain hunting and coupon clipping? Is it based on the simple wisdom of not spending more than I need to, or is it driven by a belief in scarcity, the fear of not enough? Do I feel worthy of the best?

Each of these practices calls for mindfulness to be applied in a different and unique way in your life. The key is to be present enough with your actions in the moment to witness your underlying intentions, many of which you do unconsciously. The ability to be the conscious observer of your actions will allow you to catch, challenge, and change any underlying unconscious intention undermining your ability to achieve the goal of an abundance consciousness.

Practice 2
SET CLEAR AND OBTAINABLE GOALS.

The obvious message of this chapter is that when you are focused on where you want to go, rather than where you don't want to go, that's where you end up. The question you have to ask yourself is, How much time do I spend obsessing about where I am, and any negative conditions present, rather than concentrating on where I desire to be? The practice is to remember that your primary focus becomes your reality; it is where you are instructing your mind to take you. When you get in your car, you generally have a destination in mind before pulling out of your driveway, yes? Why should arriving at an abundant, purpose-filled life be any different? Metaphorically speaking, having clear goals is like looking at a reliable road map on the highway of life before you begin the journey. While you may use your GPS to get to your chosen destination once under way, you still need to program the system with your intention—where you wish to go—before you depart.

Goal setting has been used for thousands of years to motivate and guide people toward a life worth living, so let us examine the process and practice of setting the type of goals that will be useful in accessing the principle of abundance. Consider the following guidelines as a starting point:

1. **Set clear and measurable goals.** One of the greatest ways to harness your energy and focus the power of your intention is to establish clear goals that require specific action and a timeline that produces measurable results— and write them down. The way to accomplish this is to set short-term goals (one to five months), midterm goals (six to twelve months) and long-term goals (one to three years)—each followed by a statement of what actions you will take by a certain date to bring about said goal.

2. **Be realistic.** Don't set goals that are beyond the realm of possibility. As an example, while I love adventure, at sixty-eight years of age, it would be unrealistic for me to set a goal of becoming an astronaut. Keeping your

goals "real" does not mean that you shouldn't aim high and shoot for the stars; however, it does mean your intention must be achievable in real time.

3. **Choose goals that are yours, not someone else's.** Too often, we embrace other people's ideas of what will make us happy; typically, they're the goals of those closest to us. It's difficult to get genuinely passionate about any goal that does not first originate in your own mind and heart; without passion to fuel the journey, it will be short lived.

4. **Be accountable for the goals you set.** This can be achieved by sharing your goals with a friend or mentor who you know will be your cheerleader and who is also willing to hold your feet to the fire. Do not, under any circumstance, share your goals with the "trolls"—those who will criticize, find fault with, or intentionally undermine your intentions.

5. **Include in your goals a vision of a better world for all of humankind.** Be sure that your goals carry you beyond personal and material gain. This means that you shouldn't set goals that are only self-serving; include other people as "beneficiaries" in your goals as they are reached. In other words, as you achieve your goals, can you see the world becoming a better place by means of your success?

6. **Be gentle with yourself when you fall short of your goals.** On your journey, there will be times when, regardless

of how well focused you are on your intention, things will happen that sidetrack you from your goals. While this may grieve or even anger you, once that mourning period is over, pick yourself up and continuing moving forward.

THE PAYOFF

When you understand the power of a focused mind, the results speak for themselves. Arriving at your chosen destination of an abundant life is a given when you establish and maintain a disciplined, focused mind; it will take you where you truly want to go.

Once you put your attention, your thoughts, your energy, your consciousness on a new intention, that's what you begin manifesting into your life.

—**Wayne Dyer**

Awakening to the realization that the mind makes a terrific servant but a terrible master is a major accomplishment. With it comes the power to command our lives—to shape our own destiny—unlike anything we may have ever experienced. For the one who intends to claim their power and become a conscious cocreator with a Universe that awaits their command, *anything* is possible! Being 100 percent accountable for the content of our consciousness reshapes the essence of our being, and in the process, we acquire what seems to be superhuman power wherein nothing can deter us from our mission: a life of unparalleled abundance, a life truly worth living. This is the power of our focused intention when it's sustained by our undivided attention.

However, be forewarned, creating a life of freedom and abundance comes at a cost; as Uncle Ben admonished his nephew, the newly superpowered Spider-Man, we must understand that "With great power comes great responsibility." We have to invest the time required to set our course and stay true to it, which means mindfully thinking things through *before* we take action and then moving in that intended direction with faith, confidence, persistence, perseverance, and patience . . . lots of patience. In other words, the power of a focused mind is not harnessed casually or for immediate gratification. The payoff comes in knowing that upon arriving at our final destination—a life worth living— we have mastered the power of intention, and that is the only power that will set us free.

Power Points to Personalize

- **"The mind is a terrific servant but a terrible master" is a powerful proverb.** Is your mind your master or servant? Becoming the master of your mind requires diligent present-moment awareness. Only with clarity of focus and intention can you make your mind your faithful servant.

- **A focused mind is like a laser beam;** an unfocused mind, like an incandescent light. On your journey through life, the clarity of your goal (intention) and your ability to stay focused on it (attention) ensure you will arrive where you instruct your mind to take you.

- **(Intention + Attention) x Belief is the equation for a life worth living.** You are always creating something in the garden of life; the question is, is it a manifestation of not enough or of more than enough? As with all living things, you may trust there is an intelligence within you that knows how to grow your most attentively held intentions.

- **Your mind is continually absorbing information from outside sources;** be sure it is information that affirms what you want to create. Remember, the principle of

GIGO (garbage in, garbage out) determines whether your mind will be your master or your servant. You have the power and the ability to set clear goals that steer your life where you want to go. The law of attraction is on duty twenty-four hours a day.

- **With great power comes great responsibility.** Know that the power of your intention means that you, and you alone, determine your destiny. Being responsible for the thoughts you think and the beliefs you hold sets you free to discover the secret to life. You are one with the source of all abundance.

CHAPTER SIX

Rule 5: Be in the Flow

Unlock the Paradox Found in the Law of Circulation

Nothing is static . . . Because your body and your mind and the universe are in constant and dynamic exchange, stopping the circulation of energy is like stopping the flow of blood. Whenever blood stops flowing, it begins to clot, to coagulate, to stagnate. That is why you must give and receive in order to keep wealth and affluence—or anything you want in your life—circulating in your life.

—**Deepak Chopra**

THE PREMISE

Being in the flow denotes the degree to which we consciously allow energy to pass through our lives; it's a matter of give and take. An affluent life is one that is operating within the law of circulation, inviting abundance to flow in and out of our lives in intentional and measurable ways.

Which Came First, the Chicken or the Egg?

While the rule of this chapter is "Be in the Flow," the action that facilitates being in the flow revolves around the practice of mindfully giving *and* receiving. As Ralph Waldo Emerson put it, "The gift, to be true, must be the flowing of the giver unto me, correspondent to my flowing unto him." Giving can be thought of as letting go, because that is what it requires. Paradoxically, it's quite impossible to give unless there is also a receiver, someone or something willing and able to accept what is being given. This is why being an open and willing receiver is as important as being a joyful giver. Being in the flow requires you to become skilled and graceful at doing and being both, but, as you will soon discover, there is more to being in the flow than just the acts of giving and receiving.

At the center of the paradox known as the law of circulation lingers the question, Where do I start? Which action comes first, the giving or the receiving? This paradox is also found in the old saying "Which came first, the chicken or the egg?" Whether we are talking about the chicken and the egg or giving and receiving, we have to relinquish the need to know in advance of the act which comes first. Accept that the Universe, consisting of one billion trillion stars, while still expanding at the speed of light, knows more about the principle of abundance than we do. Just as eggs have always become chickens, and chickens have always created an abundance of eggs, as we enter the flow of freely giving and receiving—or vice versa, receiving and giving—we need to trust that the Universe will reciprocate and provide for us in kind. Learning how to fully be in the flow is a lifestyle that creates affluence in our life, and it is a practice that begins by fully embracing the paradox found in the law of circulation.

THE GREAT PARADOX

Before you can manifest more of whatever it is you desire, you have to first prove to the Universe that you are capable of having it by developing a consciousness that affirms there is no shortage of that which you seek. To do this you must create a vacuum or space for what you seek to receive, and the only way you can create that space is by

letting go of what you do have while affirming that this
or something better is now flowing to you. That's the law
of circulation in action. To people enmeshed in a fear of
not enough, this logic will make no sense at all. So they
cling and hoard, which simply broadcasts a message to
the Universe that they lack, to which it responds, "Let me
help you reinforce that belief for you." To a person who is
established in a conscious awareness of his or her unity
with the source of all good, it cannot be clearer: letting
go is a prerequisite for receiving. We can do this more
easily when we trust the principle of abundance and the
law of circulation.

One of the great paradoxes in life can be found at the center and circumference of the principle of abundance. The law
of circulation affirms that the Universe is energy in perpet-
ual motion, dynamically exchanging one form of itself for
another, and that in order for abundance, in any form, to flow
into our lives, we must also allow it to flow *out of* our lives.
This dynamic exchange is a conundrum with which humankind has struggled for millennia because it seems so counterintuitive. In essence, the message is, "Letting go of what we
have is a prerequisite to receiving more of what we desire."
Let's face it, irrespective of what form of good it may be,

everyone loves receiving more, having more, and especially holding on to more, but when it comes to the letting go part of the equation, not so much. While this is a modern-day paradox with which most of us can identify, the need to make sense of—and peace with—the law of circulation is nothing new. Over the centuries the mystics and masters who understood this quagmire have taught the same "be in the flow" principle to those who had ears to hear and the heart (courage and faith) to follow their guidance. The teacher Jesus grasped this great paradox and summarized it—and the law of circulation—by clearly emphasizing the importance of being open to and in the flow (and the consequence of *not* being open to and in the flow): "By your standard of measure it shall be measured to you; and more shall be given besides. For whoever has, to him shall more be given; and whoever does not have, even what he has shall be taken away from him" (Mark 4:24–25).

If we were to translate this classic idiom into our modern-day language and metaphor, we might say it this way: Your standard of measure is the depth of your consciousness; it is done unto you exactly according to your deepest belief. Therefore, if you are aware of your oneness with the principle of abundance and believe that more than enough is available, you will be comfortably open to receiving more than enough with grace and ease. In addition, you'll be equally comfortable and open to letting the good you hold freely pass through your life because you trust and know that more will find its way to you. Perhaps this is what prosperity guru Catherine Ponder was implying when she wrote, "If you want greater prosperity in your life, start forming a vacuum to receive it." Similarly, Ernest Holmes added clarity to the wisdom of creating a "vacuum" when he declared, "There are no voids because the Universe abhors a vacuum." In other words, whatever vacuum you might create *must be filled with something.* The question is, what will that "something" be? The answer is with that which reflects your *current* consciousness—which is the law of attraction in action.

This is how the law of circulation works: If you are unaware of the principle of abundance and are ensconced in a belief in not enough, you will fail to create a vacuum because you are clinging so tightly to what you have that the law of circulation has no alternative but to circumvent you. It will flow around, over, or under you, rather than through you and your life; in the process, it will sweep what little you may have into its vortex—all because you failed to create a vacuum by which to receive. Rather than take this personally, we can embrace, with an increased level of "awareness, awareness, awareness," the lesson being offered by an impersonal principle to discover, challenge, and change whatever beliefs hold us captive in a continuous loop of not enough. Can you see the wisdom of the paradox? While this may seem more than unfair, it is nonetheless the indiscriminate manner in which the law of circulation works, especially when commingled with the law of attraction. When you decipher the key to abundance embedded in the paradox itself, your affluence (the free flow of abundance) will be instantly influenced by the law of circulation.

THE PROBLEM

What keeps us from enjoying greater affluence in our lives is fear that causes constriction; fear crimps the conduit of consciousness through which abundance flows, and the mystery of the paradox—the law of circulation—goes unexplored and misunderstood.

Life is a series of natural and spontaneous changes. Don't resist them—that only creates sorrow . . . Let things flow naturally forward in whatever way they like.

—Lao-tzu

The query we must each courageously address is, "What keeps us from forming a vacuum (letting go) that will draw an abundance of good to us . . . and with the reward of affluence so accessible, why do we avoid forming that temporary vacuum?" I say *temporary* vacuum because there are no true voids, and it must be filled with *something*—either an abundance of *more than* enough or an abundance of *not* enough; our consciousness determines which it shall be.

The ancient wisdom of being in the flow of life, as opposed to struggling against it, is not only sage, it is common sense. As Lao-tzu affirms, we must learn how to let things flow naturally forward. The operative word here is *forward*: anyone who has ever waded into a fast-moving stream knows that when you trust the current, it is much easier to let go and be naturally lifted in its forward-moving flow than to struggle against it. Fear often has us in a death grip, clinging to the rocks along the shoreline, resisting the flow, because we can't see far enough downstream to trust that life knows what it is doing and where it is going . . . and to let go. The resulting resistance becomes a habit—a way of life—that spills over into every area of our lives, and as a consequence of clinging, we suffer. That is what fear does; it *always* pushes against the natural flow of life and causes suffering.

In the East, nonresistance has been taught for millennia as a way of surrendering to the forward flow of life, trusting and knowing we are one with the current itself. In the early 1960s the practice of letting go of our attachments became popular in the West, and the saying "Just go with the flow" was coined. Coalescing with a collective desire to experience greater freedom of expression and inner peace, the term first surfaced in the newly burgeoning pop culture as an idiom signifying nonresistance and one's ability to trust, to surrender oneself to the prevailing direction and pace of the collective energy rather than push against it.

Today, depending on the altitude of one's attitude and perspective, going with the flow might be seen differently— as resignation, not caring, laziness, or taking the path of least resistance, or as simply having a laid-back, laissez-faire attitude. On the other hand, with clear intention, going with the flow could also be seen as profoundly deep wisdom, a sacred discipline practiced by those who understand their oneness with the Universe, knowing it is the source and supply of their abundance. Being in the flow is not a new idea. Throughout the ages, adherents to many disciplines understood the creative nature of free-flowing energy, as well as what is required to tap into that flow and use it to manifest abundance of every kind. However, before we can tap into the flow, we have to make sense of, and peace with, the fact that giving and receiving are two ends of the same channel connecting us to an ocean of affluence that eternally flows in (receives) and ebbs (releases). In other words, we must transcend our fear of being in the flow and trust where it takes us.

To Access the Secret to Life
We Must Unlock the Paradox

Only by giving are you able to receive more than you already have.

—**Jim Rohn**

It is only by fully understanding the importance of the dynamic exchange of energy, the open-ended relationship between giving and receiving, that we can "unlock the paradox." To create true affluence (flow), we have to first understand the secret to life—our oneness with the Universe—and prove that we understand it by embodying the wisdom found in the paradox; we can only be in the flow by letting go. For people resisting the flow—meaning those whose fear of not enough immobilizes them—this wisdom will fall on deaf ears because their attention is not on the flow at all, but elsewhere; they are so busy clinging to what they have, while also staring longingly at what they *don't* have, that the idea of letting go of what they do have never crosses their mind. This fear of scarcity transmits a distress signal to the Universe (which can only affirm their deepest beliefs) that they don't have enough, to which it responds, "Since it is done unto you as *you* alone believe—and you believe there is not enough—there is no alternative but to give you *more* of not enough."

It's important to point out that we are not talking solely about letting go of money and other material things, but also about the more intangible forms of energy we would like to have more of, such as smiles, hugs, respect, compassion, kindness, and generosity of spirit. In other words, if you want to receive a smile or a hug from others, you must prime the pump by extending one first. As a universal principle, the law of circulation does not know or care about the difference between a smile and a hundred-dollar bill; it knows only that energy in every form must flow out as well as in. For those who are clearly established in a conscious awareness of what the secret to life is—and where to find it—the message is exquisitely clear: Letting go of what we have is not an option reserved for special occasions; it is the practice of a lifetime. If we wish to establish permanency in the flow, we must let go and transcend our fear of not enough. We can do this more easily when we trust the principle of abundance by first deciphering and personalizing the paradox called the law of circulation.

THE PRINCIPLE

When we impede the flow, we block the principle of abundance from manifesting in its many forms. Creating an abundant lifestyle means consistently participating in the dynamic exchange of energy. One of the primary ways we impede the flow is by not using what we have.

Prosperity is the out-picturing of substance in our affairs . . . we must receive, utilize and extend the gift.

—Ernest Holmes, *The Science of Mind*

There Is More to the Paradox Than Giving and Receiving

As Ernest Holmes observes in the preceding quote, manifesting prosperity is a triangular process that requires the ability to receive, *use*, and release energy irrespective of what form it takes. In other words, deciphering the code to an abundant life is actually a three-step process, not a two-step process. This is an aspect that many of us overlook, and as a result, the pipeline gets clogged; we get caught up in the giving and receiving aspect and forget about the using aspect.

While accepting (receiving) and releasing (giving) are vital to the process, what happens between those two points is equally important. Mindfully *using* what is received moves energy forward and thus connects the two ends, completing the cycle. Becoming aware of whether and how you are using what you have received can serve as a litmus test to determine where you may be impeding the flow. Consider the following example as a way to discern the manner in which you may or may not be fully utilizing the things that occupy space in your life today:

Because it is so essential and something you see every day, in your mind's eye, think about your bedroom closet. Are you using *all* the clothes (shoes too) in that closet, or is it a bit cluttered because you are holding on to a plethora of clothes, hoping one day they will come back in style or that you'll lose enough weight to wear them again? Now breathe ... and take a look elsewhere around your home and observe where there is clutter in one form or another: the garage, hall closets, kitchen drawers, refrigerator, pantry, and so on. Metaphorically, this all symbolizes how you may be resisting the flow without even realizing it. As a basic rule of thumb, if you have not used something in the past year it is likely you never will. Let it go to someone who can use it. Sell it, give it, or donate it; to hold on to things you are not using blocks the flow. Does the mere suggestion of letting certain things go cause you discomfort? Does fear of not enough have you resisting the flow, clinging to things you don't use? Remember, "awareness, awareness, awareness" is the first step; it opens the portal to the present moment where your true power lies, where changing your mind and opening to the flow is possible.

Be Mindful of Your Attitude When You Let Go of Anything

When you do choose to release something, it's important to examine the mind-set with which you release. Are you letting go with a feeling of joy and an attitude of gratitude, or do you feel fear, regret, resentment, and uncertainty? Be mindful that in either case, you are emitting a signal to the Universe, which is listening twenty-four hours a day, constantly affirming what you believe to be the truth about yourself and your life. When you are cognizant of when and how you are utilizing the things that flow to you, you'll inherently see that they also have an expiration date—a life span—when it is appropriate to release whatever it is. Often, it's not that you are consciously fearfully clinging as much as you've become jaded (or bored) with it, or maybe even unaware that it is even there. Nonetheless, if you are not using it, your flow of abundance is being impeded.

Remember, everything in your life represents energy in one form or another, and energy *must* move, or stagnation sets in—and with it, dis-ease. This is why mindfulness is so important: mindfully receiving (accepting), utilizing (using), and extending (giving) the gifts that life bestows on you is imperative to being in the flow—and staying there with grace and ease.

Money Is Currency: It Must Flow to Grow

> Money is congealed energy and releasing it releases life possibilities.
>
> **—Joseph Campbell**

The same practice of staying in the flow applies to your money as well as material things. Because money plays a central theme in everyone's life, it offers us a visceral example of how easy it is to go unconscious and impede the flow without even being aware we are doing so. There is probably no single thing in our lives that has more fear-based energy wrapped around it than our relationship with money, so let's look at it with a discerning eye.

Money alone has no value; it's a paper (or metal) symbol that represents a certain degree of energy waiting to be set free—which means it must flow and be utilized. Money is a wonderful tool for processing energy if it is managed mind-fully. However, if managed poorly, it can cause much suffer-ing. What is your current relationship with money? Is money your master or your servant? In order for money to serve you, you must *use* it mindfully; it has to be moving (circulating, moving *with* the current) through your life. This is not to say that saving or investing your money is not appropriate, be-cause that is a very wise thing to do. The operative word here is *wise*. You must ask yourself: What drives you to hold on to your money? Is it wisdom or fear of not enough? Stop, breathe, and truly consider this, because how you answer is important; it may reveal where your flow of abundance is being crimped.

UNDERSTANDING THE DIFFERENCE BETWEEN WISDOM AND FEAR

More than likely you have a spare tire in the trunk of your car; no doubt, it is a very wise decision to have one. How-ever, you don't think about your spare tire every time you get in your car and turn it on; the fear of getting a flat tire doesn't automatically rise in your awareness. True wis-dom is having the tire in your trunk in the event you need it, but the fear of getting a flat tire is not dominating space in your mind. Likewise, when it comes to money, there is true wisdom in having some in reserve in the event you need it, but be certain that the fear of scarcity is not occupying space in your mind when you put that money in reserve. Why? Because, again, the Universe is listening very intently to the signals you emit.

Examine how much power you may be giving to money when, in reality, it is simply a bartering tool, a useful form of energy that you can exchange for many other forms of energy, such as food, clothes, gasoline, electricity, entertainment, a doctor's time, and so on . . . but to serve you, your money must remain in the flow. This can be accomplished by understanding that at times the line between wisdom and fear can be very thin. In those times, mindfully challenging the fear when it arises, rather than mindlessly reacting to it, is the mark of a wise person. The practice is to remember that being in the flow means wisely accepting (receiving), utilizing (using), and extending (giving or releasing) the energy of abundance irrespective of the form in which it comes to you. When you remain mindful that you are one with your source, being in the flow will happen naturally.

Keeping Your Emotional Pipeline Open to the Flow

Thoughts and emotions are energetically a higher vibration and therefore less dense than material things; they are among the most powerful forms of energy that move through you.

Because of this, it is important to be certain that your emotional "pipeline" is not clogged and that it is free of debris and clutter. If you are paying attention, your emotions have a message for you; they are continually trying to tell you what is going on in your mind, especially when you may not be consciously aware of what that is. There are many thoughts and emotions that can create sludge in the pipeline, blocking the flow, such as regret, jealousy, envy, greed, selfishness, and pessimism, which are all derivatives of fear.

Fear is the master sludge maker. We know that virtually all fear is attached to the concern of potential loss of something (or someone). When fear is wrapped around the principle of abundance, it impedes our flow of good in the future; so too will a negative emotional attachment to something or someone from the past. The one emotion that will keep you stuck like glue to the past more than any other is resentment and its cousin, anger (which is also fear in one of its most toxic, convincing disguises). When your mind is busy resentfully holding on to the past, it leaves no space in the present moment to form a vacuum, or opening, to receive anything new.

The solvent to remove the glue of resentment from the pipeline is forgiveness, which is why the great teachers throughout history have taught the necessity and practice of forgiveness as a daily ritual; it sets you free from the past and opens you to the flow of life in the present. The practice is to remain mindful that as long as you live in a human skin, there will be a need for forgiveness, even if only for yourself. Being proactive and making forgiveness a daily practice is a mark of a wise person. Being emotionally aware and honest with yourself is an essential part of the process. When your thinking and feeling nature becomes stifled, repressed, or enmeshed in fear of the future or resentment of the past, you are transmitting a signal to the Universe that it can send your abundance elsewhere because you have no room to receive anything good in the current moment. And you can be sure the Universe is listening. Forgiveness is essential if your intention is to live an abundant life.

THE PRACTICE

The law of circulation is an omnipresent principle. To mindfully witness and personalize the flow in every area of our lives is a powerful way to deepen our trust in this law.

Dwell as near as possible to the channel in which your life flows.

—**Henry David Thoreau**

Thoreau's admonishment to stay close to the flow is worth embracing. The question is, how do we "dwell as near as possible" to a principle that is already operating everywhere? Where do we start? We need look no further than our own bodies to witness how the law of circulation works for us all equally. We now know that being in the flow is a threefold process wherein it's equally important to receive, use, and release energy in any form; one is not more vital than the other. There is great wisdom in observing the many different ways that you are experiencing abundance in your life, because it's proof that you *already* have access to the flow.

CONSIDER HOW YOUR BODY DEMONSTRATES THE WISDOM OF BEING IN THE FLOW

- **Your digestive system** must *receive* energy in one form (food) and *use it* by converting it to another form (proteins, amino acids, blood, skin, hair, muscles, and so on), and then *release* what is no longer needed (waste), resulting in perfect assimilation, utilization, and elimination. Your body, in its innate wisdom, knows that to stay healthy it must honor the flow—the law of circulation. It knows that any tendency to hold on too long to what is received will impede the flow and disease will set in.

- **Your heart** is another exquisite example of the law of circulation in action. Common sense tells us that in order for your cardiovascular system to function in a healthy manner, it can't accept more blood (energy) into its chambers than it pumps out of its chambers. However, after being pumped out of the heart (releasing or giving) and before being pumped back into the heart (accepting or receiving), the blood is fully utilized, carrying needed oxygen, hormones, and nutrients to your cells and every organ in your body, as well as carrying away (releasing) waste that is flushed out through the body.

- **Your lungs** also demonstrate the trifold nature of the law of circulation. To say it is more blessed to give than to receive is like saying it is more blessed to breathe out than in. Clearly each begets the other. As you breathe in, your lungs receive (accept) the air, and your blood becomes oxygenated, circulating the oxygen necessary to produce energy throughout your body (utilizing). As you breathe out (release), you discharge carbon dioxide that if held in is toxic. Utilizing the gift of air is a vital part of the process between receiving and releasing. If you breathe in and do not release that breath, you impede the natural flow of energy, and the result is not beneficial to your longevity. Conversely, try breathing out (releasing) and not drawing in another breath (receiving), and again you'll discover your life span diminishes rapidly.

As made evident in the preceding examples, there lies in your body the innate wisdom found in the paradox called the law of circulation. Take time, as a mindfulness practice, to sit quietly and observe your body being in the flow with effortless grace and ease. What can you learn from your body and how it functions? Can you feel your faith in the flow deepening? Now begin to explore where else in your life you can apply the wisdom found in the paradox of the law of circulation. Consider that when the law of circulation is functioning correctly in your body, it delivers the energy you need to physically function in the world. Then you can convert that energy into other forms of energy, such as a paycheck, which then gets converted into another form of energy called money, which gets exchanged for another form of energy called rent or a mortgage payment, gasoline, electricity, and, yes, food to fuel your body. No doubt, the cycle of receiving, utilizing, and releasing energy—only to receive it again—is the result of being in the flow that facilitates abundance.

Practice Makes Perfect

There is abundance of opportunity for the man who will go with the tide, instead of trying to swim against it.

—**Wallace D. Wattles**

Are you ready to demonstrate your ability to mindfully "go with the tide" and enter the flow in new and intentional ways? The following list contains a few action steps you can take today to prime the pump and more fully participate in the law of circulation. Be aware of any resistance that may arise in the process of implementing these action steps. This is where the rubber meets the road!

1. Remembering that mindfulness is always your point of entry to the present moment, become the silent witness to how the flow is working in your body right now. Is energy flowing freely or is it being restricted?

   - Did you know you take in approximately seventeen thousand breaths a day? Understanding that you are demonstrating an abundance of air, as you breathe in, do so consciously. Visualize the air flowing into your lungs effortlessly and hold that breath for ten seconds, imagining how it is serving your body's needs. Then release the breath slowly and feel a sense of gratitude rising from within knowing the next breath is coming with ease. Finally, extend your awareness to your muscles. Are tension and knots in your neck, shoulders, back, or legs cutting off circulation? If so, breathe deeply and visualize each breath as it is released, carrying away that stress and tension—again, the law of circulation at work.

- Next, focus on your heart and visualize your blood circulating abundantly, accepting, utilizing, and releasing what is necessary to sustain your body in perfect health. Did you know that your heart pumps about two thousand gallons of blood through its chambers and beats more than a hundred thousand times a day? Imagine the amazing intelligence within that causes your heart to continually beat and circulate an abundance of blood without you having to tell it to do so.

- Finally, consider the meal you last ate, which at this very moment is being converted to skin, organs, blood, fingernails, and hair. Be in awe of the wisdom of your body, which knows how to honor the law of circulation by accepting and utilizing that food, and releasing what is no longer needed—and all without you telling it how to do its job. Smile and know you are not only *in* the flow, but you are also *one with* the flow.

2. Knowing that the physical surroundings in which you live offer valuable insights into your current state of being in the flow (or not), take a walk through your home and, with a discerning eye, notice where the law of circulation is possibly not being honored.

   - Start inside your home. Do your closets need to be decluttered? What message are you sending the Universe about your ability to receive? Then move to your garage.

Are things in order there, or are they stacking up in a manner that makes it difficult to feel energy flowing freely through the garage?

- After going through your closets and garage, remembering the rule of thumb that if you have not used something in the past year you most likely never will, gather everything that fits that description and make a plan to release it all. Take notice of any resistance or fear thoughts that may arise and realize how those very things to which you cling may be causing the sludge that is clogging the pipeline to a greater flow.

- Remembering that everything is energy in some form, and knowing energy has to move, consider selling or giving away things you are not using so that they may be utilized by someone else. See yourself circulating energy, clearing out the pipeline. Note: *Do not* put what you don't sell back in your closest or garage! Donate it to a worthy charity or nonprofit; *extend* it to others who can fully utilize it.

- If you really want to experience the exhilaration of fully being in the flow, consider donating some or all the money earned from the sale; give it to any of the many nonprofits that do such good work on behalf of others. If you would like to deepen the experience, consider giving your gift anonymously. There is great power in giving what is ours to give with no need for acknowledgment attached. It means you are totally free and clear in the flow.

- If you are a member of a spiritual community and are not already doing so, consider tithing to that organization. A tithe represents 10 percent of whatever financial good flows into your life; it is then given freely to the organization from which you are receiving spiritual nourishment—again, the law of circulation in action. Tithing is *not* a spiritual law; it is a spiritual *practice* that is a measurable way for you to consistently be in the flow. As with any other form of giving, our tithes should be extended joyfully and gratefully with no strings attached; tithe because you *can*, not because you "should." As we already know, nothing contaminates the flow of our giving faster than guilt or resentment. Remembering that energy moves in many forms other than just money, consider tithing as a practice that can include giving of your time and talent as well. It is a powerful statement to the Universe that you are fully invested in being in the flow.

3. Understanding that you are an "energy conduit" and that energy is channeled though your intentions and actions, consider how you are entering the flow by giving the intangible part of yourself to others.

- Prime the pump for being in the flow by offering a smile and a kind word to every person you encounter, whether at work, at home, at a restaurant, or even on the street. That small amount of energy is multiplied abundantly because it also opens you to *receive* an abundance of the same.

- Consider inviting the person standing behind you in the grocery line to go ahead of you. Offering kindness through an act of courtesy and goodwill puts you in the flow of abundance in a very subtle and rewarding way.

- Another meaningful way to enter the flow is through serving others on a volunteer basis. When you give your time to others, you offer them a gift that goes beyond material value. Consider volunteering for a local non-profit, or sharing your talent and knowledge as a mentor to young people. Being in the flow in this manner affirms to the Universe that you are open, ready, and able to receive abundance in tangible and intangible ways.

4. Knowing that energy moves through your emotional body as well as your physical body, take time daily to do a mental scan of your emotions and see where you may be impeding the flow.

- Are you holding any unresolved thoughts or feelings brought on by fear? Because fear projects you into the future (where you have no control), it can create an underlying feeling of powerlessness in the present moment that impedes your ability to access the flow.

- Likewise, is your mind stuck in the past because it is wrapped around the toxic emotion of resentment? If so, understanding that resentment clogs the flow of abundance in the present moment is essential.
- In either case, be it fear of the future or resentment of the past, remember that your oneness with the Universe (your source) can be experienced only in the present moment. Whether you need forgiveness or faith, letting go seems to be the message that being in the flow brings to us.

THE PAYOFF

The law of circulation is manifesting in your life today as either a cornucopia of more than enough or a vortex of not enough, depending on how freely energy flows through you. There are an infinite number of ways the principle of abundance can be channeled through you. It's empowering to remember that you are the gatekeeper who directs the flow.

Go into yourself and see how deep the place is from which your life flows.

—**Rainer Maria Rilke**

Are you starting to see how the principle of abundance flows in your life? At the start of this book, when we began our journey together, we clarified that our focus would not be on manifesting "things" solely at the material level. We agreed that prosperity is the logical manifestation (effect) of an abundance consciousness (cause). Whether you desire an abundance of time, love, money, respect, good health, fulfilling relationships, or (fill in the blank), the law of circulation operates exactly the same way: energy in any form must move, and your consciousness is the conductor that determines the flow wherein receiving, utilizing, and releasing are mutually necessary. Embracing this fact is vital to what happens in your life from this point forward because now you know you are the only person who directs and regulates the flow of energy that manifests as the life you call your own. This fact bears repeating: *you* are the only person who determines how abundance shall flow in, through, and out of your experience, which allows you take the onus off your parents, your children, the government, your boss, your spouse, the economy, the lottery, or even plain old luck. There is only one thing that stands between you and the secret to life, and that is your willingness to take the plunge, to be in the flow and fully honor the law of circulation.

Power Points to Personalize

- **The Universe is perpetually exchanging one form of energy for another.** In order for abundance, in any form, to flow *into* your life, you must also allow it to flow *out of* your life. The paradox of being in the flow affirms that by forming a vacuum, you are preparing to fill that void by both giving (letting go) and receiving (accepting).

- **There is more to the paradox called the law of circulation than giving and receiving;** you are also required to utilize that which flows to you. The principle of abundance cannot serve you if you do not wisely use the gifts it brings to you; you must complete the cycle between receiving and releasing. If you fail to do so, you are circumventing the natural flow, and stagnation will result.

- **Because fear always pushes against the natural flow of life, it causes suffering.** When resistance becomes a habit, it spills over into every area of your life, and the pipeline through which abundance flows becomes clogged. Knowing that the Universe always affirms your deepest beliefs, what signal are you sending now?

- **Remembering you are an energy conduit, observe the ways that you are already in the flow.** Notice how the law of circulation is currently working in your life. Then notice how you might be obstructing the flow in some areas. What action can you take to begin forming a vacuum and thereby become open to the flow of greater good?

- *You* **are the only person who determines how abundance shall flow in your life.** The law of circulation is always available to you; accessing and using it is a choice you make with every breath you take . . . and, of course, every breath you release.

CHAPTER SEVEN

Rule 6: Be Passionate

*Do What You Love: Abundance Follows
the Path of Least Resistance*

Strong emotions such as passion and bliss are indications that you're connected to Spirit, or "inspired," if you will. When you're inspired, you activate dormant forces, and the abundance you seek in any form comes streaming into your life.

—Wayne Dyer

THE PREMISE

Passion alone is neither good nor bad because it is simply an intensified energy surge that passes through us; it's what sparks that surge that matters. When you are happy doing what you love—and loving what you do—you are inspired, and passion ascends naturally from within and does the heavy lifting, opening the portal to the principle of abundance.

Passion is generally thought of as a powerful, compelling emotion or feeling about something or someone. While being passionate is most often thought of as a good thing, passion can also have a dark side if it is misguided. The deciding factor is whether it arises from love or fear in one of its many guises, such as fury, rage, envy, or jealousy. Passion driven by fear can be destructive and counterproductive to an abundant life, while passion impelled by love can be constructive and an essential component in creating a life worth living; this is why it's important to do what you love. Practicing emotional awareness can assist you in identifying and harnessing the energy created by doing what you love and then using it in intelligent, intentional, and proactive ways. Notice that when you are happy and doing what you love to do, you naturally enter the flow of life with a sense of effortless grace and ease; in this context, grace is the natural unfolding of an abundant Universe—and ease is without struggle. To enter the flow of life with grace and ease is to realize you need not force, push, pull, manipulate, or coerce anything or anyone to create a flow of abundance; you need only allow it to lift and carry you, which is what happens naturally when you are doing what makes you happy, what you love to do, what is *yours* to do.

What does it mean to do what is yours to do? Simply put, it means that when you were born, you arrived here predisposed with certain unique gifts and innate talents that were meant to be used; you came on a mission of sorts and were equipped to succeed on that mission. When you align your passion with those gifts and talents, you will have discovered that which is yours to do. This is the journey you were born to take!

Passion Gets the Juices Flowing

> Do what you love. Know your own bone; gnaw at it, bury it, unearth it, and gnaw it still. *chomp, chomp*
>
> —**Henry David Thoreau**

Perhaps the greatest reward that comes from passion is that when you are authentically passionate about your life—about what is yours to do—it opens one of the primary arteries through which universal abundance flows, which is joy. When you are motivated to do anything simply for the joy of it, you may be assured that you have arrived at the wellspring of abundance. The popular mantra "Do what you love and love what you do" is more than pithy folk wisdom; it's an entry point to the secret of life—your oneness with your source. In short, passion is the energetic umbilical cord that nourishes your soul by keeping you connected to what makes your life meaningful, happy, juicy, joyful, and fulfilling—a life worth living. As Thoreau implies in the preceding quote, when you are passionately engaged in doing what you love, doing that thing (whatever it may be) becomes to you what a favorite bone is to a dog; you know it intimately well because you *enjoy* gnawing on it and you can't seem to get enough of it. When you are truly passionate about that thing, you know you can lay it aside and later return to it feeling equally enthusiastic about chewing on it some more, loving it, focusing solely on the pleasure you derive from doing that thing. That is what passion does; it is a self-perpetuating surge of energy that keeps you tirelessly coming back for more, and always with a smile on your face. Passion and pleasure go hand in hand because when you are doing what you love, you feel good about yourself and life in the moment, and that makes it much easier to keep on keeping on with whatever it is. If you are mindful in the process of doing that thing, you will also realize that you are part of something far greater than you. In other words, when you are fully present and in the moment with your passion, it becomes the connective tissue that binds what is alive, expansive, and vital within you—the microcosm—directly to that which is equally so in the macrocosm, the Universe.

Passion is energy. Feel the power that comes from focusing on what excites you.

—**Oprah Winfrey**

Are you beginning to see the common thread running through each of the Abundance Rules? Your oneness with the Universe *is* the secret to life. When you find passion at the center and circumference of your life, it becomes the limitless power surge that lifts and carries you over obstacles, forward (in the flow), merging as one with the principle of abundance. Of course there are always a plethora of "yeah-buts" that pop up at this point in the conversation, such as, "Yeah, but what if what I love to do isn't a practical way to generate a living?" or, "Yeah, but what if what I love to do seems self-serving to me?" or, "Yeah, but what if what I love to do isn't what others want me to do?" Then, there is the ever-popular, "Yeah, but what if I don't even *know* what it is I love to do?" These are all valid questions that should not be ignored and will be explored in this chapter as well as from a different perspective in the tenth Abundance Rule, "Be a Catalyst for Good." For now, the two most pertinent questions are:

1. Are you currently doing what you love and loving what you do? If not, why?

2. Are you willing to let go of that which is *not* yours to do— and may never have been—and embrace that which *is* yours to do?

If these questions cause your heartbeat to quicken, that is a good thing; it means I now have your attention!

THE PROBLEM

Just blindly following your bliss is not wisdom; it is naïveté. Intentionally merging your passion with your purpose is a mindfulness practice that has to be balanced with a plan that requires teamwork between your head and heart.

If passion drives you, let reason hold the reins.

—Benjamin Franklin

In moving toward a life worth living, you'll inevitably come upon a three-fingered fork in the road where "should do" and "inspired to do" intersect with "can do." Which path shall you take? The choice will depend on how well your head and heart communicate.

- **"Should do"** is driven by reason (or logic). Reason is a good thing and is necessary for our survival; it is also an appropriate moral compass to consider duty, commitments, and the choices we make. However, when "should do" arises obsessively from a sense of guilt or shame (and it often does), it stirs resentment that, as we know, creates emotional sludge that only blocks the flow of abundance. Perhaps most important, when reason gets clouded and we become obsessed with a concern of loss or fear of making a mistake that may affect us downstream, it immobilizes us.

- **"Inspired to do"** originates purely from the heart and is driven by a desire that stokes the fire of a fearless passion. This is a good thing because without passion, life becomes perfunctory and meaningless. However, "inspired to do" can also have an extremely short attention span. When unguided, it's easy for passion to turn a deaf ear to the voice of reason; left to its own devices, "inspired to do" can easily wander off the pathway of good intentions in pursuit of instant gratification and get lost forever, never to be heard from again.

- **"Can do"** is the middle path that brings reason and passion together; clearly, we need both if we are to move toward a life of abundance, purpose, and meaning. Ben Franklin's advice to let reason hold the reins is spot on; we need passion *and* reason, and balance is the key. While nothing may slay our passion quicker than when we (or others) obsessively apply "should do" to our desires, it's equally true that allowing our passion to go unchecked is like riding an unbridled high-spirited horse: we'll likely not end up where we desired to go. There is a fulcrum—a point of balance—between passion and reason that must be sought and that leads to "will do." Too often, we allow our heads to get in the way, and it blocks us from following our heart; yet, as we can clearly see, passion alone is not enough. There needs to be a plan that honors both.

(Reason + Passion) x Commitment = Success

Passion, though a bad regulator, is a powerful spring.

—**Ralph Waldo Emerson**

One of the greatest dangers in touting the importance of doing what you love and loving what you do is that it tends to resonate with that part of us that thrives on instant gratification. Unfortunately, many people reading self-improvement and prosperity books believe that all they need to do is think positive thoughts, quit that boring job or leave that stagnant relationship, and run off and join the metaphorical circus—doing what they love—and the money, success, and happiness will come magically pouring down like rain. Sorry, but it generally doesn't happen that way. Passion is best served with a large dose of patience and sometimes humility as well. Just because you may have great passion for something—and you love doing it—it doesn't necessarily mean you are great at it, yet. Often time is required to develop your gifts. Irrespective of how deep your passion may run, you will still need to be equipped with the necessary tools (and perhaps credentials) to do that thing well, and it may require an investment of your time and resources such as going back to school, getting credentials in a certain field, or hiring a mentor in your field of choice. This is where the wisdom of balance between head and heart comes in. The good news is that if you have the passion for doing that thing, you are halfway home! With commitment *and a plan* (which will be more fully covered in the tenth Abundance Rule), just about anyone can learn the various vocational or life skills necessary for success, but the one thing that you can never be taught is how to be passionate about the thing you love; either you feel it or you don't—and if you don't, you would be well advised to seek your fulfillment doing something else. Billionaire Richard Branson articulates this point:

> Ideally, since 80 percent of your life is spent working, you should start your business around something that is a

passion of yours. If you're into kitesurfing and you want
to become an entrepreneur, do it with kitesurfing. Look,
if you can indulge in your passion, life will be far more
interesting than if you're just working. You'll work harder
at it, and you'll know more about it. But first you must
go out and educate yourself on whatever it is that you've
decided to do—know more about kitesurfing than anyone else. That's where the work comes in. But if you're
doing things you're passionate about, that will come naturally.

Passion Generates the Power
but Reason Points the Way

Passion plays a crucial role in creating the life you dream of,
but passion alone is not enough; it needs to be directed by
reason. Without passion your boat is dead in the water; you'll
be like a sailboat with no wind to move it. But equally important, without reason (logic) to chart the course and hold
the rudder steady, the wind of passion can easily blow you off
course and onto the rocks. Again, this doesn't mean there
may not be rigorous training or education involved in acquiring and honing the proper skill set, but because passion is
driving you—rather than dragging you—the process can be a
joyful one. Reason and passion go hand in hand; reason sets

the compass that points the way, and passion puts wind in the sails that get you there.

Whose Dream Are You Pursuing?

Don't ask yourself what the world needs; ask yourself what makes you come alive. And then go and do that. Because what the world needs is people who have come alive.

—Howard Thurman

Each man has his own vocation; his talent is his call. There is one direction in which all space is open to him.

—Ralph Waldo Emerson

While obtaining the proper tools necessary for success must be a priority, at the same time, it is not wise to spend precious time and resources learning how to do something you don't love doing just because it may be lucrative; your heart will not let you get away with that for too long. There is perhaps no more important Abundance Rule than "Be Passionate," because without passion, even the most worthy vision of a life worth living will never fully come to fruition; it will be dry and lifeless. Too often passion gets thrown out the window in the name of practicality and people-pleasing. All you need to do is ask anyone who has followed a personal path motivated not by their own deep passion and interest but by the desire to create wealth or satisfy the needs, wishes, or dreams of another person.

I have personally known many people the world might label as "successful" who, after a number of years, simply quit their careers because *one thing* was missing—and it wasn't the money; it was the joy and satisfaction found in doing their work. They didn't like—let alone love—what they were doing. The happiness factor was missing. What they discovered was that they were pushing a rock up a hill, trying to do what really wasn't theirs to do. As an example, in my early days as a music teacher, I witnessed more than one child take piano or guitar lessons not to pursue their own passion for music, but to make their parents happy. As you might guess, their attention waned quickly because they found no joy or fulfillment in playing. It was interesting that eventually the parents of those kids would have to drag them to class, while the kids who loved playing couldn't get there fast enough. Obviously, when you love what you do, the thing you do loves you back.

There is another passion-killing land mine that lies buried

just below the surface of many people's conscious minds that keeps them from actualizing their greatest joy and happiness; it is a close cousin of "should do" called "must do." Shades of the puritan work ethic are alive and well in the "must do" mind-set because it is not passion that drives one's actions but rather a belief (often unconscious) that suffering and depriving oneself of any pleasure is a noble act that somehow gains God's favor. The idea that suffering is a prerequisite to success is erroneous thinking, not to mention archaic. The logic is, work hard *now* even if you don't enjoy it, suffer deeply *now* even if it hurts, and if you endure long enough and are very lucky, you'll collect your reward *later* in the hereafter. In other words, postpone your happiness until after you are dead and then you'll have eternity to feel better about feeling bad *now*. In the "must do" mind-set, passion is so deeply repressed that given enough time, it goes comatose and then flatlines. Clearly, there is a direct correlation between passion, joy, and happiness.

Happiness is a derivative of joy, which is what we feel welling up from within the core of our being in any moment when we are completely aligned with, plugged into, turned on, and tuned into "Life," which can happen anytime, anywhere, because it is not reliant upon external conditions. Happiness is the horn by means of which authentic joy trumpets Spirit's presence in the human condition, and it really is an inside job.

> *—The Art of Uncertainty: How to Live*
> *in the Mystery of Life and Love It*

Nothing will throw a wet blanket on your happy dance faster than trying to accomplish something that doesn't have *your* name inscribed on it. Becoming clear on whose life you are living and whose favor you may be trying to gain is an affirmative step that moves you further into the flow of abundance. Be passionate about your life and prove it by doing what *you* love and loving what you do. Remember, the Universe is waiting for a sign from you that says, "I am an open and receptive channel through which abundance flows with grace and ease." The sixth Abundance Rule, "Be Passionate," assures you that when you can align reason (mind) with passion (heart), intelligently doing what you love and joyfully loving what you do, abundance will be there to meet you at the finish line.

THE PRINCIPLE

Energy in any form will follow the path of least resistance. Passion is energy that naturally follows that path because when you are doing that thing you love to do, you are in the flow. You are not pushing energy—you are being effortlessly lifted and pulled by it.

Non-resistance is the key to the greatest power in the universe.

—**Eckhart Tolle**

It has been said that in a contest between a river and a rock, the river always wins. Why? Because the river is willing to take the path of least resistance, going over, under, around, and eventually through the rock to its destiny, which is to ultimately merge with the ocean. The rock is stuck where it is, relentlessly pushing against the river, resisting the natural flow of water until, over a long enough time, it's worn down to a pebble. If you ever visit the Grand Canyon you'll see evidence of this. Simply put, water flows downhill because it cannot resist the call of gravity. Similarly, abundance flows where it is least resisted; passion points the way and carves the path for abundance to follow. Ask yourself, Am I more like the river or the rock today? The answer is easy to discern—just look at the amount of resistance to life you may feel. Are you pushing a rock up the hill? If so, consider getting in touch with doing what you truly love and witness how passion rises and washes over you.

Many pundits in the self-help camp vehemently oppose the philosophy of taking the path of least resistance. Perhaps they believe that hard work and strenuous effort are a prerequisite for creating a successful life; there may even be some residue lingering unconsciously in their beliefs from the previously mentioned puritan work ethic. It may be because they confuse effort with intention. The obvious question this tees us up for is, If hard work is the secret to a prosperous life, why isn't everyone who does hard work prospering? Let us be clear—there is an immense difference between "hard work" and "working hard." *Hard work* is usually thought of as laborious, tedious, and stressful—as if pushing to get something done or make something happen— and often arises from the "should do" or "must do" mind-set. On the other hand, *working hard* has a completely different motive that is energizing, is driven by a vision, and arises naturally and enthusiastically from the "inspired to do" mind-set, which lifts you into the flow with grace and ease.

In other words, when passion is fueling your intention, it really isn't an effort at all; it's a joy. Even if it requires working hard, you can be assured that happiness has your back.

The Universe Is on Your Side, but You Still Have to Do Your Part

At the moment of commitment the entire universe conspires to assist you.

—**Johann Wolfgang von Goethe**

What if the Universe really is conspiring for your success? What if by intentionally doing what you love and loving what you do, you are enabling the Universe to do its part? A word of caution: Do not be lulled into thinking that passion (working hard) alone is the magic bullet that will save you from having to do your part, because it is not; it's also about working smart. So, what is your part? Perhaps it's time to redefine what that is. Just as water following the call of gravity cannot resist flowing downhill, when you are intelligently and passionately engaged with life in the present moment, following the call of that which is yours to do, you are not resisting the flow; you have harnessed and become *one with the flow*. Your part is to wisely discern what brings you the most joy in life and, as Goethe says, *commit to it* by setting an intentional, intelligent plan in motion to get you there. This is when what Deepak Chopra refers to as the "law of least effort" becomes your best friend and servant.

THE PRACTICE

When you are engaged in the moment, doing whatever it may be that generates a feeling of joy and happiness, mindfully pause and look closely between the cracks of your bliss and you may discover something: that thing that is uniquely yours to do—what you were born to do—hiding there awaiting your recognition.

Nature's intelligence functions with effortless ease . . . with carefreeness, harmony, and love. And when we harness the forces of harmony, joy, and love, we create success and good fortune with effortless ease.

—**Deepak Chopra**

Is it really possible to use your passion as a guide that points you toward a life of purpose and meaning, doing what you were born to do? Can you actually create a flow of abundance in your life simply by doing what you love? The mind obsessed with logic and reason often scoffs at such a possibility because it is addicted to the idea that hard work must drive the bus, but think about it: when you are doing what you love and loving what you do, the boundary between work and play magically becomes invisible because your motivation is not just to be rich or even successful—it's to be fulfilled, joyfully expressed, and happy; the material reward is an afterthought or effect. As Deepak Chopra implies in the preceding quote, success and good fortune effortlessly follow in the vortex of passion when it is moving in an intelligent and productive direction.

Your Passion Will Help You Discover That Thing That Is Yours to Do

If you don't know what your passion is, realize that one reason for your existence on earth is to find it.

—Oprah Winfrey

Your work is going to fill a large part of your life, and the only way to be truly satisfied is to do what you believe is great work. And the only way to do great work is to love what you do. If you haven't found it yet, keep looking. Don't settle. As with all matters of the heart, you'll know when you find it.

—Steve Jobs

Earlier in this chapter, two vital questions were posed: How will you know when you are doing that which is yours to do, and once you know, will doing that thing be a practical (logical) way to generate a living? First, if you are like most people, you probably love doing *many* things. However, there are a number of telltale signs that will appear when you are doing that one special thing that sets it apart from the others. Being particularly mindful of these signs when they pop up is essential. It's one thing to do what you love and quite another thing to be crazy, head-over-heels *in love* with what you do. As an example, there are many people in my life I *love* being with, but I am passionately, crazy, over-the-moon in love with my wife, Diane, and therefore, I can't be with her enough (hopefully she feels the same). Can you see the role your passion plays in connecting you to that one thing that is calling to you more than anything else?

Second, let us keep in mind that the Universe doesn't know or care what practicality is. Being practical is a human bias concocted to establish a baseline that separates so-called reality from dreams. Practicality is often based on judgment, fear, rigidity, shortsightedness, and the collective opinion (consciousness) of others. Often when we hear someone say, "Oh, get real," what they are really saying is, "Oh, climb down from that lofty dream you have." What is it about the "dreamers" in life—people such as Walt Disney, the Wright brothers, Leonardo da Vinci, and so many others—who broke through the barriers that others referred to as "reality" and in the process opened the doors to new frontiers? They didn't do what was "practical"; they did what they were passionately in love with—they did that which was theirs to do and were wildly successful. Yes, they worked hard, but it's unlikely they ever said it was hard work. Again, abundance and success in any endeavor is drawn into the vortex of passion.

The moral of the story is, as a universal principle, abundance doesn't flow to what is deemed practical; it follows the path of least resistance and flows to the greatest open receptacle, which in this case is a creative mind and a passionate, willing heart. Remember, at the end of the day, it's not really a living you want to generate but something much bigger—a way of life centered on wholeness, self-expression, harmony, joy, and love. With this in mind, consider the following points, which can help you determine if what you're doing is your true passion and that which is yours to do:

1. **Time passes quickly.** It has been said that time stands still when one is in love. Notice that when you are engaged in doing what you truly love and loving what you do, you lose all sense of time; the minutes turn into hours without a second glance at the clock, and you are always amazed that you have been at it for so long.

2. **You are tireless and have boundless energy.** Remember, passion is an energy surge. When you are doing what you love and loving what you do, your passion ignites and becomes the fuel that drives you both emotionally and physically. Even when you are finished doing "that thing," you will feel a sense of satisfaction that is already wooing you back for more.

3. **You will be inclined to use your natural talents.** You arrived on this planet hardwired with specific gifts and talents that were meant to be developed and shared with the world. Passion is the motivating force that brings those gifts and talents forward simply because you "in-joy" expressing yourself.

4. **You would (in theory) do it even if you didn't get paid.** Consider professional athletes and entertainers. While they usually are extremely well paid for what they do, most of them would admit that they would still do it even without such great monetary rewards. Why? Because

they don't do it *just* for the money; they do it because they *love what they do.* In the words of billionaire Oprah Winfrey, "The reason I've been able to be so financially successful is my focus has never, ever for one minute, been money."

THE PAYOFF

Following your passion will allow you to discover that which is yours to do in life; your passion will set you free from the tyranny of a joyless and unhappy life. You will unearth and bring the gift of your authentic self to the party called life.

Doing what you love is freedom. Loving what you do is happiness.

—**Lana Del Rey**

When you tap into your passion you will be using the natural momentum of an expanding Universe to enter the flow of abundance. Staying connected to your passion will make your life richer, deeper, and more meaningful. As you may remember from chapter one, the secret to life can be found only by venturing beyond the safety and comfort of the known. The greatest adventure of your life begins the day you give yourself permission to follow the vision that arises from your heart—and remember, the heart knows no boundaries; it craves freedom.

Doing what you love and loving what you do may require you to go where you have never gone before—especially if it meets with the skepticism or disapproval of others—but the freedom that comes with the risk is a reward beyond measure. Discovering that which is yours to do *and then doing it* is an act of courage that truly will set you free, and at the end of the day, isn't that what we all truly seek—the freedom to do that thing we were born to do? Celebrate your passion and pay attention to it because it points the way to the abundant life you so richly deserve.

Power Points to Personalize

- **Passion is an intensified energy surge that passes through you;** it's what you do with it that matters. When you are happy, doing that which is yours to do, your passion naturally lifts you into the flow of life, where the principle of abundance awaits you.

- **Passion and reason must work as a team.** Practicality alone will smother the burning embers of passion, while creativity and passion unguided by clear reason (intention) can go completely off the rails. Discerning the difference between "should do," "inspired to do," and "can do" will help guide your passion.

- **Passion will always follow the path of least resistance.** There is a difference between hard work and working hard. If your path is laborious and stressful and you feel like you are pushing a rock uphill, it is likely that passion is missing from this endeavor. When passion is fueling your intention, it's a joy, even if it requires working hard. Abundance follows a joyful heart.

- **The Universe will support you, but you have to do your part.** Discern what brings you the most joy in life and then set an intentional, intelligent plan in motion to get you there and commit to its implementation. Pay close attention to what stimulates passion in your life—watch for the telltale signs—and become proficient at doing that thing. Abundance follows passion, but it requires a plan that integrates that passion with a clear intention and vision.

- **After discovering that which is yours to do, do it.** Once you realize you are free to follow your passion, you will be guided to your greatest good because you will be doing what feeds your mind, your heart, and your soul. In the process, your life will open to new possibilities, allowing you to explore beyond the safety of the known and go where you may have never been before. Loving what you do and doing what you love is why you have come—and now the fun begins. Can you feel it?

CHAPTER EIGHT

Rule 7: Be Blessed

*Practice the Power of Positive Perspective
by Focusing on What's Right with Your Life*

Be grateful for small things, big things, and everything
in between. Count your blessings, not your problems.

—Mandy Hale

THE PREMISE

*There is a difference between counting your blessings and
knowing you are blessed. This is the power of perspective.
Knowing you are blessed originates in your heart, with a
simple awareness that you are blessed with the gift of life.
Counting your blessings happens exponentially as you
awaken to your oneness with the principle of abundance
and see it manifesting in your daily life.*

At this point on our journey through the first six Abundance Rules, we have established that we exist in an expanding Universe and that the impartial principle of abundance is an inherent attribute of that expansion. In addition, we know that we are all energy conduits, and as such, we direct that impartial flow of energy in a manner that reflects our most deeply embodied thoughts and beliefs, resulting in an experience of a life filled with an abundance of either not enough or more than enough. This is why the seventh rule, "Be Blessed," is so important; it invites us to witness the many different ways the principle of abundance operates in our lives and in our world. Let us begin by clarifying what the words *bless* and *blessed* mean and the awesome power they carry.

Depending on the context, to *bless* can mean to consecrate, dedicate, glorify, honor, venerate, magnify, endow, confer on, give to, or have favor with or grace upon. To be *blessed* can mean to receive, give thanks for, be grateful for, show appreciation for, or know and accept one's own good fortune.

Most of these definitions can be found in any dictionary. Whether they are being used as a verb or an adjective, the words apply to you and the life you are here to manifest. Some, all, or none of these definitions may resonate with you; nonetheless, they all carry the energetic imprint of abundance. In this chapter we shall explore how and why this is so. To bless and be blessed is a beautiful and beneficent endowment of energy that affirms one's own true worth. In the context of *The Art of Abundance*, as a verb, *to bless* is the act of consciously directing affirmative energy in a very specific manner. To bless someone is to confirm that wholeness exists in every area of their life, from the tangible to the intangible—to see that person through the lens of an abundance consciousness, knowing nothing is missing. As an adjective, to be *blessed* describes a consciousness that affirms that whatever our personal perceived needs may be, they are already filled because of our oneness with the source; the blessing simply puts our seal of agreement on this idea and confirms it so. In other words, both knowing we are blessed and blessing others acknowledge our ability to see an infinite Universe—and therefore an infinite supply—as the sacred sustaining life force in that which is blessed. The actual blessing is manifested the moment it arises in our awareness, knowing and accepting it is so.

> The more gratefully we fix our minds on the Supreme when good things come to us, the more good things we will receive, and the more rapidly they will come; and the reason simply is that the mental attitude of gratitude draws the mind into closer touch with the source from which the blessings come.

> —**Wallace D. Wattles**

A positive perspective on life matters; being blessed and *knowing* you are blessed are two different things. Do you see yourself as blessed? Your blessings are legion; however, you may completely miss the most obvious ones if you are looking solely on the surface of life, at the material world. As an example, you have already been exquisitely blessed beyond measure, beginning with the ultimate gift: the gift of life. The question is, how often do you consciously pause to reflect upon and appreciate that blessing? The gift of life is beyond any monetary value—it is priceless; yet we seldom consider this fact. This is an important point to ponder because, as you know, the more energy you focus on any one thing, the more life force flows to it, expanding your experience. When you bless yourself (or anyone or anything else), you are using the power of a positive perspective to direct the impartial energy of the Universe in a very personal, conscious, specific, and beneficial way.

In this chapter we shall explore a number of ways to actualize abundance through the process and practice of conscious, intentional blessing. There is nothing magical or mystical about conferring a blessing—anyone can do it. One need not be a minister, rabbi, holy person, or saint; one need only be conscious, present, and aware that one's blessing recognizes the presence of goodness and the sacred oneness of life. However, before you can effectively bless anyone or anything else, you must be able to see and accept how blessed *you* already are; only then can you pay it forward. In other words, as the ancients would say, paradoxically speaking, you can't give something you don't have. Pay close attention to the seventh Abundance Rule, "Be Blessed," because when you master the power of positive perspective, you'll realize that to be blessed and *know* you are blessed will enable you to become an authentic blessing to others, which in part is why you are here. This is when the secret to life—knowing you are one with your source—becomes a true demonstration of abundance, because it affirms that you know there is more than enough for everyone.

THE PROBLEM

Being blessed is not something you have to earn; you already are abundantly blessed. The challenge is that those blessings will never be actualized as long as you are obsessing over what appears to be missing or wrong with your life.

We can always choose to perceive things differently. You can focus on what's wrong in your life, or you can focus on what's right.

—**Marianne Williamson**

It's easy to become mesmerized by the drama being played out daily through the media; it's so compelling to watch, it can be addictive. However, if we are not mindful we can unknowingly become part of the drama's cast because the law of attraction is on the job at all times. The theme of the drama, which is deeply ensconced in the collective consciousness of humankind, seems to generally be about focusing on what's wrong with our lives rather than what is right. Because there are so many variations on this theme it systemically bleeds over into just about every area of our life. The tendency is to silently gawk at other people's good fortune (their perceived blessings) and compare it to what we believe is missing in our own lives. When we are consumed with looking for what is wrong with our body, our significant other, our children, our neighbor, our lifestyle, our job, our financial status, our politicians, our country, our world, or our (fill in the blank), it's easy to overlook what's right.

The truth is, even if we aren't consciously aware, the majority of us are so profoundly blessed that we have become jaded. This is when hedonic adaptation kicks in without our conscious awareness. Also known as the hedonic treadmill, it describes the single-minded pursuit of something that we don't have but are consumed with having, solely because we think that once we have it, it will make what we believe is wrong with our lives right. Then, once we've accomplished or obtained this one thing, our interest slips away and it becomes just another item thrown on the heap of discarded blessings we have taken for granted and no longer appreciate, which leads us to pursue the *next* newest and best blessing on the treadmill—and on it goes. It's as if we need to continue hitting the reset button on our happiness. One often-cited example of hedonic adaption is lottery winners. Studies have shown that within a year or so of winning the lottery, they are no more happy than they were before they bought that winning ticket. As my friend and colleague, Dr. Patrick Cameron, once told me, "It seems that many people can never get enough of what they don't really need, while the true blessings in life, such as love, friendship, inner peace, and the time to enjoy them, are inexhaustible and accessible every moment of every day."

There is no question that it may be difficult to feel blessed when we are addicted to the drama of "what's wrong," but be forewarned, as author Paulo Coelho admonishes, "Every blessing ignored becomes a curse." In other words, when we fail to gratefully recognize and celebrate the blessings we do have, they seem to go to waste; they tend to wither up and fall away because there is no affirmative energy wrapped around them, which is the glue that holds them in place. We have to remember, all energy (as with any form of energy, such as electricity or water) is impartial and follows the path of least resistance, meaning it can bless us or curse us, and it all depends on our perspective. Ralph Waldo Emerson offers us timeless advice on how to maintain the altitude of our attitude when it comes to our perspective: "Never lose an opportunity of seeing anything that is beautiful; for beauty is God's handwriting—a wayside sacrament. Welcome it in every fair face, in every fair sky, in every fair flower and thank God for it as a cup of blessing."

Focusing on our blessings initiates a centripetal force—a gravitational pull—that attracts a self-perpetuating cycle of good, drawing more of it to us, if we can be disciplined enough to find deep satisfaction and contentment with the blessings we have rather than dissatisfaction with what we don't have. Easy to say, but difficult to do? Not once we understand how the principle of abundance responds to a grateful heart.

THE PRINCIPLE

Because you are one with a Universe that is expanding by its very nature, when you bless something, you are instructing the Universe to enlarge upon it. The practice of a lifetime is to make blessing your life a daily ritual, knowing that in so doing, you are accessing and directing the principle of abundance in a very proactive manner.

What you focus on expands, and when you focus on the goodness in your life, you create more of it. Opportunities, relationships, even money flowed my way when I learned to be grateful no matter what happened in my life.

—**Oprah Winfrey**

Perhaps the most resourceful tool you were given to create a life of purpose and meaning is the mind you are using now to read these words. With this mind you can think and, at the same time, observe the thoughts you are thinking. Self-awareness is an amazing gift because it allows you to witness, challenge, and change errant thinking. Understanding that your core values and beliefs shape the thoughts that become the things most important to you, it's crucial to examine and challenge any beliefs that sponsor thoughts that separate you from the abundant life you desire to manifest. Ask yourself, "Do my thoughts tend to focus on what's wrong in my life or what's right in my life?" Be honest with yourself because your future depends on it. Become the impartial observer of your own thinking process and see where it leads you. As a brief self-inquiry process, answer the following:

- Do you find yourself staring at what seems to be wrong with your life (the drama)? If so, know that doing so separates you from an abundance consciousness. You can't obsess over what's wrong and expect to attract what's right.

- Can you rejoice in other people's success? Remember, envy and jealousy (judgment) separate you from the flow of your own potential for abundance. Celebrate everyone's success knowing there is enough for you and them.

- Do you ever criticize the rich? If so, there is a place in your mind that personalizes it—as if you are criticizing yourself. If you bless others, there is a place within you that also feels and receives that blessing—as if you are bestowing a blessing on yourself. In other words, the same judgment you inflict upon others you also inflict upon yourself. As found in the Scriptures, "Judge not and you shall not be judged." Trust that each person is subject to the effect of their own consciousness.

Understanding the Power of a Positive Perspective: Are You Looking Up or Down?

Two men look out the same prison bars; one sees mud and the other stars.

—**Frederick Langbridge**

If you discover that you are looking down rather than up, breathe, smile, and affirm, "This is the day I take my mind back to basic training at Camp Consciousness." As you were growing up, you received basic training from others on what to think, but you most likely were never taught how to think; there is a vast difference between the two. The content of your mind and how it functions are two entirely different things—and they need to work together. Growing up, few people were ever told that the altitude of their attitude would affect their entire life—that their mind-set, the sum of their beliefs and perspective on life, would ultimately shape their reality. Most of us grew into adulthood with no idea we'd played a part in creating that reality, which is why the victim mind-set is so prevalent in our culture. If this topic pushes any buttons for you, reread the third Abundance Rule, "Be Accountable for Your Consciousness." When it comes to developing an abundance consciousness, it is never too late to have a do-over.

Reshaping Your Consciousness Begins with Building an Attitude of Gratitude and Then Going Beyond It

Building a belief system that supports the vision of the life you desire to manifest begins—but does not end—with an attitude of gratitude. As Plato wrote, "A grateful mind is a great mind which eventually attracts to itself great things." Training your mind to focus on the good in your life begins with the practice of conscious gratitude because it primes the pump for a flow of abundance. Teachers have long taught the necessity of self-reflection through the mindfulness practice of journaling—one form of which is focusing daily on your blessings and what you are grateful for by writing it down. While journaling is a powerful practice, many people find it is difficult to do on a daily basis because it requires time and commitment. Is there another way to stay anchored in an attitude of gratitude—perhaps an easier way that would take us beyond a few weeks of good intentions? What would be required of us to go *beyond* gratitude? Perhaps the range of our focus needs to be expanded to include not just our many blessings but also how much we tend to take for granted. The reality is, most of us take nearly *everything* and *everyone* for granted on a very regular basis.

I point out the fact that we tend to take so much for granted because it's simply a fact of life that often unintentionally slips below the radar; however, I also point it out as an invitation to pause and look deeper. When we begin to consciously focus on the abundance of blessings that life lays at our feet every moment of every day, an attitude of gratitude will ascend from the core of our being. With the correct perspective, training ourselves to become aware of what we are taking for granted can prime the pump for the flow of abundance. Life is fundamentally good and the abundance

that lingers behind unexpressed gratitude lies in smiling re-
pose, waiting for us, if we are but willing to be present in the
moment and see the blessings present there.

THE PRACTICE

*When we begin to look beyond our obvious blessings—
between the cracks and crevices of our daily life—we begin to
see with new eyes, eyes that are able to perceive infinite grace
and the principle of abundance operating in exquisite and
subtle ways. Again, the power of a positive perspective opens
the portal of plenty by igniting an attitude of gratitude.*

Can you see the holiness in those things you take for
granted—a paved road or a washing machine? If you con-
centrate on finding what is good in every situation, you
will discover that your life will suddenly be filled with
gratitude, a feeling that nurtures the soul.

—Rabbi Harold Kushner

The next breath you take, hold it in as long as you can. Then
notice how grateful you are as you release it for the next breath

to follow (yes, the one you were taking for granted). This may seem like an extreme example, but it makes the point that most people don't appreciate what they are used to having until it is gone. When was the last time you actually paused and gave thanks for your next breath? Consider this: the very first thing you did when you arrived here was to take a breath in, and the very last thing you will do when you leave here is to breathe out; it is the countless breaths (and moments) between those two points that you tend to take for granted—and *every* breath (and moment) is a priceless blessing and gift. I use this example to illustrate how easy it is to lose sight of how blessed you already are. Becoming aware of what you may be taking for granted each day can become a life-changing practice.

To expand upon this point, before reading any further, consider just *one thing*—other than your next breath—that you may have been taking for granted. At first, your mind may scramble to find just the perfect place to start the process; this is because it's quite easy to unknowingly slip into a subtle sense of complacency when you get caught up in the daily "doing" of life. When this happens we tend not to notice the obvious. The tendency for all of us is to take the obvious gifts in our life for granted.

Consider the following examples as a mindfulness exercise to help you deepen your awareness of the abundant blessings already existing in your life.

1. When you last showered, washed your body, and shampooed your hair, did you consider the blessing of *having* hair to wash, let alone the soap and warm water with which to do so? We seldom do. Now that you are aware of what you may have been taking for granted, during your next shower, observe the sense of gratitude that naturally arises as you step into the flow of warm water and suds up your hair and body. You are literally being showered with a positive flow of energy that is blessing you in a most subtle and tactile way. Enjoy it and then give thanks for it! Are you beginning to see how the principle of abundance is always present and available in places you least think of looking for it? Remember, the power of a positive perspective primes the pump for a virtual plethora and flow of good in every area of your life.

How about your amazing earth suit that houses and sustains your soul?

2. How often do you consider the blessing your physical body is with all of its many components: your legs, feet,

arms, fingers, eyes, liver, heart, brain, lungs, kidneys, etc.? How often do you take them for granted? As obvious as they may be, we seldom take time to consider the many critical body components so necessary for our existence, let alone thank them for doing such amazing, selfless, tireless work for us, day in and day out, since the day we were born. At first it may sound a bit odd to be thanking your liver for doing such a great job, performing its unique duty, assisting in the digestion of your food and purifying your blood—but each time you acknowledge that you have been taking your liver for granted, what you are doing is sending it a silent blessing. In other words, you are automatically thanking it for a job well done—and don't believe for a minute that your liver doesn't benefit from your positive perspective and thoughts. The same could be said about your heart, lungs, and every other organ holding life force. Your body responds favorably to the positive energy you direct toward it. Being mindfully aware that you have been taking your body for granted invites you to pause, breathe, and be present with it in the moment. Try it and notice how abundantly alive you suddenly feel.

What about the people and the planet you take for granted?

3. Consider your doctors, nurses, ministers, and first respond-
ers who are there when you need them . . . and the dedicated schoolteachers to whom you entrust your beloved
children . . . and the people who collect and recycle your
trash . . . and the gardeners who maintain the beauty of the
planet. Don't forget about your employers, employees,
friends, neighbors, and cherished spouse and other family
members who, too often, you tend to take for granted as
well. How about the farmers who grew the food you ate
this morning and the truck drivers who delivered it to market? And let us be sure to also remember the sun that shines
upon those crops and the rain that nurtures their growth.
What about the furnace that heats your house or the bat-
tery that started your car this morning, and the country
in which you live and that you call home?

These are some of the ways you are being blessed every
day that can be easily taken for granted if you are not mindful. Can you see the principle of abundance flowing in,
through, and as all the aforementioned things? And, equally
important, are you beginning to understand how much the
Universe really does conspire for your good?

The more often we see the things around us—even the beautiful and wonderful things—the more they become invisible to us. That is why we often take for granted the beauty of this world: the flowers, the trees, the birds, the clouds—even those we love. Because we see things so often, we see them less and less.

—Joseph B. Wirthlin

Clearly, there is a virtual cornucopia of things and people we tend to take for granted. It seems to be true that the more often we see these people and things, the less we truly *see* them; they become invisible, part of the background of a life we take for granted. When we can own this fact and live mindfully with an awareness of what we take for granted, gratitude rushes in to fill the gap between head and heart, mind and soul, and in the process, life becomes a sacred continuum of blessings. The preceding mindfulness exercise illustrates just how easy it is to become so enmeshed in *doing* life that we forget, as mentioned earlier, the greatest blessing of all: being alive. When taking life for granted becomes the norm, gratitude gets pushed aside and the exquisite sweetness of having been given an unknown, limited amount of time on this amazing planet goes unnoticed and unappreciated.

To squander the gift by not taking time to honor its giver engenders a sense of entitlement, which in turn spawns complacency and a self-centeredness that is endemic in our culture. Our world deserves better from us, and being stuck on that hedonic treadmill is not how we bring the best of ourselves to the world. As we live mindfully, being consciously aware that we are one with the source of all life, our perception changes; we begin to see, as Rabbi Kushner calls it, the holiness (blessings) in the things that we may have otherwise been taking for granted. This is when abundance becomes our divine right and the practice of blessing ourselves and others becomes a lifestyle. *Knowing* we are blessed is a way of going beyond gratitude and consciously walking a sacred earth every day of our lives, breathing in and breathing out, mindful in every step of the sacred gift contained within the breath, within the moment, and within ourselves, trusting and knowing abundance follows a grateful heart.

Make Maintaining a Positive Perspective a Mindfulness Practice

Following are a few simple action steps you can take that will help you maintain a positive perspective by consciously blessing yourself, all people, and all things. Remember, when you bless anyone or anything, you are recognizing their oneness with the source of all life, where the principle of abundance originates. Where can you begin blessing life today?

Bless your body . . . Bless your family . . . Bless your home . . . Bless your neighbors . . . Bless your workplace . . . Bless your employer . . . Bless your coworkers . . . Bless your teachers . . . Bless those who serve you . . . Bless those you serve . . . Bless your competitors . . . Bless your spiritual community . . . Bless your automobile . . . Bless the roadway . . . Bless your country . . . Bless the sun . . . Bless the rain . . . Bless the economy . . . Bless the gift of music . . . Bless the present moment . . . Bless the planet and everyone on it . . .

Now that we have primed the pump, what else can you add to the list? Take a few moments right now to do so:

_____

_____

_____

_____

THE PAYOFF

To be blessed and know you are blessed is to affirm that you are a whole person, that there is nothing missing, irrespective of conditions or the opinions of others. This is when you become a blessing to your world, and an opening for abundance becomes the norm in your life.

I am larger, better than I thought;
I did not know I held so much goodness.
All seems beautiful to me.
Whoever denies me, it shall not trouble me;
Whoever accepts me, he or she shall be blessed, and shall
*   bless me.*

—Walt Whitman

Are you beginning to see the principle of abundance operating in your life in ways that you may not have noticed before? Being blessed and knowing you are blessed is a game changer because you are seeing your life though new eyes. Practicing the power of perspective by focusing on what's good and what's right will change your life in ways that benefit not only you but also your world. When you initiate a flow of abundance in your life, it will automatically spill over into the lives of others; you cannot actualize your own blessings without also splashing some of your good on others. The practice is to be mindful that the moment you begin to focus on what's right with life—with yourself and with other people— you are transmitting positive energy that transmutes as a blessing for all concerned. It cannot be any other way; it's simply the law of attraction in action. In the words of Nigerian author Ifeanyi Enoch Onuoha, "You were not just blessed for yourself, you were blessed to be a blessing to others."

Being blessed and knowing you are blessed go hand in hand. The takeaway for the seventh Abundance Rule, "Be Blessed," is simple: because you are one with the Universe, you are *already* blessed in countless ways. The quintessential question is, what shall you do with those blessings? With an awareness of how blessed you are comes responsibility and a deepening of what it really means to live an abundant life. True abundance goes far beyond possessing material things; living in true abundance means existing in a state of mindfulness that affirms your life itself is the ultimate gift, a blessing, a pearl of great price because its value is beyond measure. Now breathe, smile, and offer great thanks to the giver of the gift, knowing you really are blessed.

Power Points to Personalize

- **To *be* blessed and to know you are blessed are two different things.** You were born abundantly blessed, but those blessings will lie dormant within until you recognize and activate them through the power of positive perspective. How you choose to see yourself and the world is where the blessing begins.

- **If you are continually focused on what appears to be wrong with your life, you overlook the blessings found in what's right.** The tendency is to then climb aboard the hedonic treadmill, chasing what you perceive to be missing, which only takes you further away from a true abundance consciousness. Make it a practice to look up, rather than down; look for what's right and you'll find the blessing in it.

- **Remember that what you focus on expands.** Examine and challenge any beliefs that lead to compulsive thoughts that separate you from an abundance consciousness. Clarify and embody your core values, beliefs, and blessings because they shape the thoughts that become the life most important to you.

- **You can train your mind to focus on what's right by going beyond gratitude.** Consider the multitude of blessings you *already* have but tend to take for granted, such as a healthy body, joyful relationships, your car (or bicycle), and the roof over your head. Train your mind to look for what's right with your life and the world, not what's wrong!

- **To know you are blessed is to know you are whole, that nothing is missing.** Practicing the power of positive perspective—focusing on your oneness with life—enables you to become a blessing to your world, initiating a flow of abundance that spills over into the lives of others in countless ways, demonstrating that there is indeed more than enough for everyone.

CHAPTER NINE

Rule 8: Be of Service

Enter the Flow of Abundance by Serving Others

When you are able to shift your inner awareness to how you can serve others, and when you make this the central focus of your life, you will then be in a position to know true miracles in your progress toward prosperity.

—Wayne Dyer

THE PREMISE

There is no better way of initiating the flow of abundance in your life than through the act of serving others. To serve is to extend your essence—your energy—to others in a manner that enriches and makes their lives better. Your intention (motivation) in serving others sets the precedent for how that energy shall return to you, as we now know it must.

Once upon time a student came to his master and said, "Teacher, you speak of the importance of selfless service to others as a way of life; you say that if I am to create a rewarding, joyful, and abundant life for myself, I must first learn to serve others. However, I am uncertain about what that means and how to accomplish it. How do I serve others and still take care of my own needs? I would like to understand the difference between selfishness and selflessness and the consequences of both."

In a dream state, the master guided the young student to a large enclosure with two doors. He opened the first door and invited the student to look in. Throughout the room were numerous large round banquet tables. At the center of each table sat an enormous pot of soup; it smelled so wonderful, it made the student very hungry. Sitting around the tables were people who were complaining and crying; they appeared weak and emaciated, as if they were starving. Each was bound to a chair and holding a long-handled wooden spoon, which, fortunately, made it possible to reach into the pot of soup at the center of the table and take a spoonful. However, because the handle was far longer than their arms, they could not get the spoons back to their mouths before the soup spilled out of the spoon, so there they sat, starving and complaining. The student was visibly upset at the sight of their anguish and suffering.

The master then took the student to the second room and opened the door. The room appeared to be precisely the same as the first. The same large round tables filled the room, each with the same pot of soup at the center of the table. The people were bound to their chairs and equipped with the same long-handled spoons, but one thing was different: here the people appeared well fed as they energetically laughed and talked with one another. The student said, "I don't understand. Why are these people so filled with joy?" "It is simple," said the master. "You see, in this room, the people have learned to consider the needs of others first—and to serve those needs, by selflessly feeding *one another* with their long spoons. In so doing, they are in turn equally well fed. However, in the first room, the people are very self-absorbed, selfishly thinking only of themselves. They are so obsessed with serving only their own needs, the idea of serving others has never crossed their minds. The answer to the question you asked about the difference between selfishness and selflessness is simple: one is 'me-thinking' and the other is 'we-thinking' . . . and the consequences of both are obvious."

This parable of the long spoons has been used as a teaching tool for many years. While the source of the original story is uncertain, there are numerous variations on the theme; this version is embellished in a manner that makes it relatable to the eighth Abundance Rule. The essential message is quite obvious: serving others is a vital part of living on planet Earth if we wish not to just survive, but to thrive. Simply put, if your desire is to live a whole, healthy, happy, and abundant life, serving others is not really an option; it's a prerequisite. What's of significance is the mind-set, manner, and intention with which you serve. Shifting from "me-thinking" to "we-thinking" is one of the surest ways to affirm that you have discovered the secret to life—your oneness with the Universe, a.k.a. the source of all abundance.

In this chapter we will begin to deepen our understanding of "being of service" as not just something we may be required to do for others while at our workplace, but a way of life, a way of walking in a sacred and abundant earth. The reality is that serving others comes with the job of being a whole human. When we live with clear intention, serving others is as natural as breathing because our motive is not driven by the ego or by an expectation of receiving anything in return; this is what makes our service selfless. Selfless service is a state of consciousness that connects one person's heart to another's; it determines the manner in which we approach everyone and everything we do.

Do you have a preconceived idea of what being of service to others is or isn't? Does the notion of serving others appeal to you or repel you? Does it energize you or exhaust you? Is your focus more on being of service *to* others or being served *by* them? An abundance consciousness calls for a mindful balance of both. If you discover that your me-thinking overshadows your we-thinking, a quick review of the fifth Abundance Rule, "Be in the Flow," would be advisable, because it will remind you that giving and receiving are two ends of the same stick. The takeaway is the understanding that serving others is a form of giving, and that doing so solely to facilitate reciprocation is not advisable because, as we know, giving—in any form—with strings attached contaminates the gift. As with the law of giving and receiving, it is wise to be mindful of the intention (motivation) that drives your desire to serve others—is it selfishness (self-serving) or selflessness (self-giving)? Make no mistake, in either case, the results will directly correspond with the intention.

Whether we are at work, at home, at the supermarket, in church, taking a walk, or even driving our car, the opportunity to be of service lies directly in front of us every day; we simply have to be present in the moment to see it. When we begin to serve others mindfully, with an understanding that we are doing more than simply exchanging one form of energy for another, just for compensation or to benefit ourselves, something profound happens: our perception of what matters shifts and our service becomes selfless. It means that, regardless of what we are doing, we approach others with respect, reverence, kindness, compassion, patience, tolerance, generosity, joy, and love, with no strings attached. The sole intention of selfless service is to be the conduit through which life is made better for all concerned. Authentic selfless service comes from an elevated state of consciousness that transcends hidden agendas and the intention of serving only for material gain. With this awareness we know we are serving others not just because we can profit from it, but because it's how we deepen our sense of oneness and connection to life; it comes with the privilege of living in a human skin, knowing and remembering we are blessed.

The question of what constitutes selfless service and what doesn't is an appropriate one to ponder, because depending on one's perspective, the same act of service could be interpreted several different ways, which is why clarity of intention is important. Do you remember the practice of "awareness, awareness, awareness" as discussed in the second Abundance Rule? If you are aware and pay close attention to your intention when reading this chapter, you will discover that the opportunity to selflessly serve others always lies before you. It will be disguised in ways that will surprise, energize, and lift you into the flow of abundance awaiting you the moment you turn your me-thinking into we-thinking. If you are present in the moment and aware, you'll discover that life is eternally providing you with abundant opportunities to be of service.

THE PROBLEM

When we approach life believing there is not enough for everyone, the human tendency is to focus on serving ourselves first, which breeds the contagion of selfishness, which reinforces the consciousness of lack, which then reaffirms the belief in not enough . . . and the cycle goes unbroken.

When we quit thinking primarily about ourselves and our own self-preservation, we undergo a truly heroic transformation of consciousness.

—**Joseph Campbell**

The collective consciousness of humankind is so deeply ensconced in the belief in not enough that its gravitational pull has sucked billions of unaware people into a vortex of lack wherein the focus on self-preservation has become a way of life. The desire to preserve and protect one's own life (and all that it contains) is not a bad thing; we are all hard-wired to do so. However, when self-preservation is driven by fear, it can quickly manifest as selfishness without our conscious awareness. The will to survive is incredibly persistent, and the more mindful we are of how covertly it operates in our lives, the more quickly and efficiently we can harness that energy and redirect it in a manner that serves (and prospers) us and our world in plentiful and positive ways.

As we begin to embody the secret to life—our oneness with the Universe and therefore with each other—being of service to others will take on a whole new meaning. There is great wisdom to be found in the saying "There is only one of us here," because it changes everything; it alters the entire landscape of our minds and hearts. Awareness of our oneness with life enables us to enter the flow with a sense of freedom; it allows us to witness the principle of abundance in action as it moves in and through us as we mindfully serve others.

By What Means Do You Measure Your Life? ✓

Service is the measure of greatness . . . Nearly all of our controversies and combats grow out of the fact that we are trying to get something from each other—there will be peace when our aim is to do something for each other. The human measure of a human life is its income; the divine measure of a life is its outgo, its overflow—its contribution to the welfare of all.

—William Jennings Bryan

As counterintuitive as it may seem to the egocentric, me-thinking mind (which is primarily focused on "self" survival), by selflessly serving others (we-thinking) we naturally shape an abundance consciousness that affirms, metaphorically, that there is more than enough "soup" for us *and* everyone else—and not just at our table (our immediate lives), but in the entire banquet hall (planet). Before reading any further take a moment to do a scan of your interior beliefs and emotions about what has just been stated. How do you measure your life? As William Jennings Bryan describes, is it by what flows *into* the sphere of what you consider a life worth living, or by what flows *out*? To go deeper into this question, how do you really feel about the idea of serving others? This is a call to practice self-honesty—and an important question to ask yourself—because your ability and willingness to embrace service as a way of life plays a major role in creating an abundant life for yourself as well as for others.

It is here that one might say, "Yes, but it is my job to serve others; I am in the service industry and it's how I earn a living. How can I serve others with no strings attached when I *expect* to be compensated for my service?" Here is where your consciousness, equanimity, and the power of intention come in. As mentioned earlier, the same act of service can be perceived several different ways. The difference between generic service and selfless service is not necessarily found in the action alone; it is the energy of intention wrapped around *any* act. As an example, if you are serving others as a way of making a living, ask yourself, "In my work do I serve my customers with reverence, joy (generosity of spirit), no judgment, gratitude, respect, patience, and consideration for that person's highest good, sincerely placing their needs before my own in the moment?" If your answer is yes, irrespective of what your job may be, you may be assured that you are serving selflessly. The happy result is that because you are *giving* your energy in a selfless and generous manner, you are automatically lifted into the flow of abundance without even trying . . . and, as we already know, what goes around comes around.

Rising above the collective belief that there is not enough to go around happens the moment we begin to lift our own consciousness from me-thinking to we-thinking. We don't have to convince the Universe that we are worthy and capable of prospering greatly through the simple act of being of service to others; we need only convince ourselves. This, then, is the "problem" we were born to transcend, and the principle of abundance waits patiently for our acceptance that there is enough because we fully know we are enough.

THE PRINCIPLE

Any form of giving with no strings attached puts us directly in the flow of abundance, which must come full circle. Likewise, being of service is a priceless gift—a specific form of energy—which, when extended to others unconditionally, places us directly into the flow of the abundance. In short, we cannot serve selflessly without also being served.

The more generous we are, the more joyous we become. The more cooperative we are, the more valuable we become. The more enthusiastic we are, the more productive we become. The more serving we are, the more prosperous we become.

—**William Arthur Ward**

The unintended silver lining that comes with selflessly serving others is that it benefits us as well. Selfless service initiates an interesting chain of cause and effect; it inherently engenders and strengthens our sense of oneness with something larger than us, which builds our self-confidence, which raises our self-esteem, which ultimately deepens our innate self-worth. Logically, then—understanding how the law of attraction works—in this chain of cause and effect, by serving others we are shaping an abundance consciousness that ultimately must draw greater good to us. In this chapter you will notice that the collective essence of the first seven Abundance Rules is integrated in the eighth, "Be of Service." As previously mentioned, the practice of selfless service begins with remembering the secret to life (your oneness with the source, the Universe). With awakening to the fact that you are one with life comes many perks, privileges, and responsibilities; being of service to others aligns you with all of them.

Serving Others Mindfully Is a High Calling and Should Be Viewed Not as an Obligation but as an Honor

Being one with life means you are privileged to share that life with every other human being and sentient creature on the planet for a precious, limited amount of time. How you spend that time will define you as either a me-thinker or a we-thinker; it will either elevate your understanding of whole-ness and your oneness with the source, or it will pull you into a vortex, creating a sense of separation from the source. With this awareness, the perk found in serving others becomes obvious: because we all come from, and share, the same source, we can say metaphorically that we are all drawing soup (sus-tenance) from the same bowl (source). As in the parable of the long spoons, because we are all sitting around the same infinite table of oneness, you can't serve without also being served. As Ralph Waldo Emerson wrote, "It is one of the most beautiful compensations of this life that no man can sincerely try to help another without helping himself." Logi-cally, then, understanding the law of cause and effect, when you serve another person, you initiate an impulse of energy that in some manner must return to you—*if you allow it to.* This means that to make the gift of serving others complete, you must also be open and willing to *be* served. Are you willing to allow others to serve you, and if so, with what attitude do you receive their service? Remember, the altitude of your at-titude matters! Some people are very uncomfortable being served, perhaps because they feel unworthy, or because it creates a sense of obligation to return the favor. By being gra-cious and grateful when being served, you honor the giver.

From a practical perspective, serving and being served is a very symbiotic process. Because you have needs, as everyone does, someone *must serve you* in some manner for you to continue to exist on the planet; as John Donne wrote in 1624, "No man is an island." In other words, in the sea of humankind, at our deepest level of oneness, we all touch and need one another. What you may need is food from the farmer, new shoes from the cobbler, or medical care from the doctor. Then again, what you may really need in this moment is genuine love and compassion from a family member, a caring smile from a neighbor, an encouraging word from a coworker, or a door held open for you by a stranger. All of these require a "provider" to serve that need. Can you see it? We fill one another's needs by being of service *to* one another *and* by being willing to be served *by* one another. This is the economy, ecology, and energy of humankind in motion; as a result, the law of circulation finds another suitable conduit through which to flow: you! The quintessential question is: How shall you serve in a manner that honors the life you have come here to live?

THE PRACTICE

To be of service is to be a conscious, open, and willing conduit through which good flows—and it doesn't happen just between the hours of nine a.m. and five p.m.

You are not here merely to make a living. You are here in order to enable the world to live more amply, with greater vision, with a finer spirit of hope and achievement. You are here to enrich the world, and you impoverish yourself if you forget the errand.

—**Woodrow Wilson**

As previously stated, selfless service is a way of life; there are as many ways to serve others as there are stars in the night sky. There is no time or place when the opportunity to be of service isn't staring you directly in the face; if you are present in the moment and willing to see the opportunity, you will. The key is to remember that it's not so much what you are doing as a service as it is the mindfulness with which you serve. In other words, function and form may be two separate things that, with clear intention, can come together as one in the present moment. As mentioned in the fifth Abundance Rule, being in the flow means having the freedom to trust, let go, and know that wherever you are and whatever you are doing aligns you with the principle of abundance. There is great wisdom to be found in the saying "Find a need and fill it," because it provides endless opportunities not only to make money but also to make a difference! Whether you are at work, at home, sitting in an airplane, standing in a line at the store, or walking the dog, when you make yourself present and ask, "How may I serve in this moment?" the answer will appear right before your eyes. Remember, selfless service doesn't have to include larger-than-life accomplishments such as discovering a cure for a major disease or creating a nonprofit organization; just be mindfully present in the moment, find a need that has your name on it, and fill it! The following is a list of only a few examples of what selfless service could look like in your life:

Find a Need and Fill It

1. By washing the dishes, taking out the trash, cleaning the garage, or filling your loved one's car with gas *without being asked*, you are selflessly serving.

2. By helping someone with special needs to cross the street, assisting a child with a homework assignment, or mentoring a young person, you are selflessly serving.

3. By volunteering time at a local hospital, homeless shelter, hospice, elder care facility, or in your own spiritual community, you are selflessly serving.

4. By making dinner for your family, mindfully remembering that you are not just feeding them, but *blessing* them, you are selflessly serving.

5. By inviting the person behind you in line at the grocery store with only a few items in their cart to go ahead of

you, or allowing another person to take that cherished parking spot closest to the store, you are selflessly serving.

6. By picking up trash or broken glass and nails along the sidewalk or road so no one is injured, you are selflessly serving.

7. By listening silently without judgment to a friend, spouse, child, or stranger as they vent their sadness, fear, frustration, disappointment, or anger, you are creating a safe place for them and selflessly serving.

8. By remaining mindful while at work that what you are doing not only generates a paycheck for you but also enriches the lives of those who enjoy the product or service you render, you are selflessly serving.

Now it's your turn. In what other ways might you imagine yourself selflessly serving others, filling their needs? List a few below:

_____

_____

_____

_____

_____

_____

Clearly, the preceding list of ways to serve could go on indefinitely. As a mindfulness practice each day, list three new ways in which you can imagine yourself serving others. Remember, they don't have to be "big" gestures of service—only sincere, with no strings attached. The Universe has no concept of big and small; it only receives the energy of your intention. As you add to your list, realize that you are also aligning with the principle of abundance as it naturally flows in you and through you.

THE PAYOFF

When we serve others selflessly, we are recognizing them for their essential value, recognizing that they matter. When someone knows, at the core level of their being, that they matter, they are intrinsically guided to demonstrate it in ways that ultimately serve others . . . and the circle is complete.

Non nobis solum nati sumus.

(Not for ourselves alone are we born.)

—**Marcus Tullius Cicero**

If you are mindful, you will see that at the center of all acts of authentic selfless service lies the sweetest realization of all: recognition. It is not self-recognition, but rather recognition of the true self that lies within every human being, waiting to be seen and honored. In the words of author Richelle E. Goodrich, "Service is a smile. It is an acknowledging wave, a reaching handshake, a friendly wink, and a warm hug. It's these simple acts that matter most, because the greatest service to a human soul has always been the kindness of recognition." We all have an innate desire to be seen, to know that who we are—and what we *do* with who we are—matters. To mindfully serve and to be served are the connective tissue that unifies us and affirms that we are all one and therefore essential to one another's existence and well-being; in other words, we truly do matter to one another. As Cicero implies, you were born to serve not just your own needs but those of your fellow humans.

We are all sitting at one of the two tables in the banquet hall of life; the question is at which one will you be seated from this day forward: At table number one, with those unhappy people who are focused primarily on serving themselves (unsuccessfully) with their long spoons, or at table number two, where those who are seated are joyfully drawing their sustenance from the same bowl of universal good by serving one another with the same long spoons? Your consciousness ensures your place at the appropriate table, and it just so happens that the soup du jour is abundance. It would be a shame not to share a large bowl.

Power Points to Personalize

- **To serve is to extend your essence—your energy—in a manner that enriches and makes other lives better.** Your service becomes selfless when you put others first, knowing that you are doing more than exchanging one form of energy for another to benefit only yourself.

- **Lift your consciousness from me-thinking to we-thinking.** As a result, you rise above the collective belief that there is not enough to go around. We-thinking also affirms that you have discovered the secret to life: your oneness with the Universe, a.k.a. the source of all abundance.

- **Serving and being served are necessary to each other.** Whether your need is for shoes, food, or a loving hug, it requires you to be open to a provider serving that need. As a result, the law of circulation is activated and the energy of abundance flows freely.

- **The opportunity to be of service lies before you in every moment.** It's not just what you are doing as service that is important—it is the mindfulness with which you provide the service. As you find a need and fill it, you are sending the Universe a message that you are open and willing to be in the flow of abundance.

- **Who you are—and what you do with who you are— matters.** To mindfully serve others is to recognize and honor them as worthy recipients of the greatest gift you have to offer: your essence, respect, reverence, kindness, compassion, patience, tolerance, generosity, joy, and love. Knowing that what goes around comes around is just an added bonus!

CHAPTER TEN

Rule 9: Be Courageous

*Seek New Horizons and Be Willing
to Risk, Fail, and Risk Again*

If we want truly extraordinary vision then [we] have
to continually expand [our] horizons, take risks. If we
don't push our edge we'll never expand our view. It's
not trespassing to go beyond your own boundaries.

—Dewitt Jones

Cherish your visions and your dreams as they are the
children of your soul, the blueprints of your ultimate
achievements.

—Napoleon Hill

THE PREMISE

The principle of abundance awaits those who are willing to come to the edge of their own perceived boundaries and courageously venture beyond them. Those who do so are the visionaries, explorers, and risk takers who believe that beyond the horizon and safety of the known lie endless opportunities wherein anything is possible.

Human beings have always been irresistibly drawn by the mystery of the unknown—that mystical place just beyond the field of their human vision. Those who were both curious and courageous enough were compelled to explore that mystery, guided by not just their human vision but an inner vision—a vision of the possibilities that lie in the unknown—while those who lacked that vision stayed behind. Before setting out on their journey they invariably looked to the expansive canopy of stars above and the horizon below—that far-off place where the sky and earth appear to commingle—as a reference point to mark their bearings. They realized that if they wanted to conquer new horizons and discover the treasures to be found there, it would require great courage; they had to take a risk—to be willing to move away from the comfort and safety of their current place in life and toward the unknown territory that lay before them, far beyond what the eye could discern as a "safe place." The challenge is, and has always been, that being *enchanted by* new horizons and *moving toward* them are two different things.

The horizon calls to each of us. There is something in our hearts that knows there is more to know, more to do; it beckons us to come closer and see what we have not seen before—to experience an expanded dimension of life and find meaning and purpose in being alive—but what is it that stops so many people from ever embarking on that trek? At this point in our journey through *The Art of Abundance* we know that creating a life worth living doesn't happen by accident, nor in the comfort zone of a semi-awake state of consciousness.

Metaphorically Speaking, There Are Three Categories of People in the World

1. Those who make things happen. They are path makers, who carve their own path and shape their own destiny and fortune.

2. Those who sit on the sidelines watching those who make things happen and then follow their lead. They are the path takers.

3. Those who wake up just long enough to say, "What happened?" and then go back to sleep. They are unaware that the path even exists.

- Category one is represented by the fewest people because of the inherent risk involved in taking the lead—loss is possible, often more than once. Relatively speaking, this is why so few people on the planet experience absolute abundance. The unwritten rule, "The more you desire to have, the more you have to risk losing," seems to sideline the majority of people; few are willing to take risks because of the possibility of loss that comes with the action. However, keep in mind, the principle of abundance does not encompass only material gain. Having an abundance of *anything* that enriches your life—whether relationships, career opportunities, personal time, hobbies, a healthy lifestyle, or (fill in the blank)—requires some degree of uncertainty and the possibility of loss. If this statement causes your pulse to race a bit, that may be a good thing; it means you are ready to at least look at what being a path maker means.

- Category two is represented by the vast majority of people because while they may be interested in exploring new horizons that lead to abundance and prosperity—essentially an enriched life—they are not necessarily committed to the process that gets them there; they are more comfortable with having others point the way and taking the risk (exposure) first. Mistakenly, they believe there is safety in numbers and that by commingling and traveling with the masses, following a well-trodden path, their risk of loss is minimized. While at times this may appear to be the case, as we shall see, nothing could be further from the truth.

- Category three is represented by those who have fallen so deeply under the spell of a belief in not enough that the idea of being a path maker—or even a path taker—is beyond their ability to imagine, so much so that they may not even realize there is a path! For them, motivation is nonexistent; to climb out of their box of complacency and explore the horizon of possibilities is just too risky. This is because they have no vision of their own; they allow others to do their thinking for them. They passively agree with whatever beliefs are being fed to them by the media or those around them regarding their destiny and ability to succeed or fail. Between the effort required to clarify a vision and set out on a path of their own making and the risk involved in doing so, the mindset is, "Why try at all?" In an odd way, it's quite easy to justify one's situation, finding comfort in knowing they can't lose what they never really had. It's much easier to stay securely ensconced in the rut of the known, where, while it may be less than rewarding, it's predictable and presumably "safe." Metaphorically speaking, they are content with consuming the scraps left behind by others who have set out on the journey.

Which Are You Today?

There have always been path makers, path takers, and those who never venture onto the path. Which are you? Can you see the role your individual consciousness plays in answering that question? The collective consciousness of humankind tends to overlap between categories two and three, causing those in category one to stand out—to stand alone. Some scientists say that our minds are innately wired (programmed) to dissuade us from taking any kind of action wherein we could hurt ourselves or suffer loss, thus discouraging risks—a primitive self-survival mechanism of sorts. If there is any truth to this, those who are path makers have found the override switch. While the admonition, "Lead, follow, or get out of the way," may be quite curt, it clearly illustrates this point.

Path makers are leaders; they are few and far between because they have the courage to transcend and break free of the gravitational pull of the collective consciousness. Path makers know it's risky to go where they have never been before, where there is no known, proven, and safe way ... *but they still go*. T. S. Eliot exquisitely summarized this mindset when he wrote, "Only those who will risk going too far can possibly find out how far one can go." This chapter is dedicated to helping you understand how far you can go on the path of your own choosing. The ninth Abundance Rule, "Be Courageous," is a call to action that will put you on the path of your own making. But, *you* have to be willing to lead the way. Are you ready?

THE PROBLEM

Inherent in every human being is the desire to expand their horizons, to know and express greater freedom, but most people ignore, deny, or in some other way repress that impulse. What they fail to realize is that it is the Universe calling them to higher ground, to see and then actualize the life of their dreams.

Most men lead lives of quiet desperation and go to the grave with the song still in them.

—Henry David Thoreau

As previously stated, many people avoid becoming path makers because of the risk of loss, whether it be five minutes from now or five years from now. The problem with avoiding taking risks is that in doing so, we really do lose something: our sense of freedom to choose our own destiny—to fulfill our own greatest purpose and potential—and without that freedom, a vital part of us dies and life becomes more about surviving than thriving. Being courageous doesn't mean having no fear; it means having the passion (heart) to risk moving forward in spite of that fear. The moral of the story is, the less risk you are willing to take, the more constrained your life will be, and therefore, metaphorically speaking, the less likely it is that you will ever discover the song within you that you were born to sing.

Being courageous opens the door to change, growth, expansion, and the principle of abundance. By their very nature, courage and risk taking go hand in hand; one complements the other. Any undertaking that requires courage automatically implies that there is a risk of loss of some sort involved; otherwise there would be no need for courage. That is what courage is: doing something that is, well, risky, and might end in failure. The irony is, even getting out of bed in the morning comes with a risk. There are countless things that could cause you to incur loss between the time you get up in the morning and the time you go to bed at night. However, the reason it usually doesn't require intentional courage to get out of bed in the morning is that you have done it thousands of times before; therefore, your mind is flying on autopilot and faith—lots of faith. The same can be said about driving your car or any other thing you do on a regular basis—while you may be taking risks, you don't dwell on them.

Taking Risks Is Not the Problem

Risk taking isn't the problem, because you do it every day; it's the *conscious fear* of risk taking that is the problem. Think of that. You take hundreds of risks every day without a second thought because you have proven to yourself over and over that the rewards to be gained by taking certain actions are greater than the risk of loss. These actions become so unconsciously rote that courage takes the day off, waiting to be summoned for "special" occasions—especially first-time occasions—when fear is most likely to raise its snarling head. At the end of the day, fear is always the culprit that keeps you from moving to higher ground, where a life of purpose, meaning, and abundance can be found and actualized. Remembering that virtually all fear stems from a concern over potential loss, let us discern what some of those special occasions might be, when calling forth our courage is the appropriate choice to make.

- **Fear of making mistakes:** Any person who has never made a mistake has never ventured very far off the well-trodden pathway of conformity. Too often we avoid being a path maker or path taker because we fear that by stepping outside our comfort zone we may make a mistake. So, we settle in for the duration and, as Thoreau says, we end up leading lives of quiet desperation. The problem is, living our lives with an inner knowledge that there is something greater awaiting us, and not pursuing it, causes great silent suffering that ultimately reveals itself outwardly. Part of the problem is a belief that mistakes are a bad thing—and that is simply not true. The key is to learn from your mistakes, to see them as gift-wrapped opportunities for either an educated do-over or guidance from your wisdom-self informing you of what not to do again, ever. Either way, it requires courage and wisdom to learn from your mistakes. With the right perspective your mistakes can serve as your master teacher and inspiration for growth.
- **Fear of rejection:** No one enjoys being rejected, and because of this, many people never take the risk necessary

to move forward. The fear of rejection is a toxic energy that spills over into every area of our lives; it restricts the flow of abundance in subtle ways we might not normally consider. How many new and wonderful relationships have never come to fruition because someone held back extending themselves to another because they feared the rejection of not being welcomed or desirable enough? How many new and amazing career opportunities or college educations have been missed because someone didn't even apply because they feared being rejected and labeled as not smart enough? How many new songs have been left unsung and how many new paintings have never been hung because someone feared the rejection of not being talented enough? Can you see the fear of "not enough" revealing itself in all these scenarios? Transcending the fear of rejection means courageously knowing that because you are one with the creative Universe and the principle of abundance, you are *more* than enough.

- **Fear of failure—as well as success:** Many people never venture beyond the boundary of their limited beliefs because they fear the risk of failing at something that might offer them the freedom to create an entirely new life. Perhaps what really keeps some of them from claiming the freedom that lies just on the other side of their fear of failure is a far more subtle fear—the fear of success. Succeeding at something great *and not feeling deserving of that success* is a land mine that lies buried in the subconscious; just as with the fear of making a mistake, sooner or later it will be unearthed and create great suffering. Once again, this is where the "not enough" syndrome reveals itself. If one's self-worth is low, it creates an invisible "hole in the soul" through which any possibility of manifesting and maintaining a life worth living escapes. Transcending the fear of failure—or the more subtle fear of success—requires the courage to examine your own self-worth and redefine who you are, based on a higher standard of truth. You are not a mistake; you were placed here on purpose, to succeed at being a unique, one-of-a-kind expression of life. Being courageous means being willing to take the risk in believing that this is true—and following its lead. (Note: If you would like to explore more deeply what being a unique, one-of-a-kind expression of life means, I encourage you to read my book *Your Redefining Moments: Becoming Who You Were Born to Be.*)

THE PRINCIPLE

Anytime you step into the role of path maker, you are telling the Universe you have faith in something larger than yourself that responds to your deepest beliefs. Being courageous is an action step—an affirmation that you know you are one with that "something" and are inviting its expansive energy to move through you, lift you, guide you, protect you, and lead the way to a joyful and abundant life.

Life shrinks or expands in proportion to one's courage.

—**Anaïs Nin**

In which of the three categories discussed at the beginning of this chapter do you currently fit? Are you a path maker, a path taker, or the one who exists in a semi-awake state of mind with no awareness of the path? Remember, you can fool yourself but you can never fool the universal (and impartial) law of cause and effect. It is important to note that there is nothing at all wrong with being a path taker, one who follows the path maker. Likewise, it's perfectly fine to be the one who never sets out on any path—but the law of cause and effect demands that the rewards (effects) in life are always commensurate with the actions (cause) taken. Irrespective of the life you live today, the quintessential question is, are you willing to believe that the possibility of a deeper, richer, more fulfilling, more fully expressed and abundant life may be waiting for you just beyond the horizon of your current reality?

Remember, you live in an expanding Universe that is continually creating new possibilities. The key is to consciously accept where you are today, bless whatever your life looks like—both the good and the less than good—and then make a commitment to courageously move forward, toward the next peak, one step at a time, remembering that the principle of abundance always follows the arc of the principle of expansion. As Anaïs Nin says, whether your life shrinks or expands depends upon your willingness to be courageous.

It's All About Heart

What your heart thinks is great, is great. The soul's emphasis is always right.

—Ralph Waldo Emerson

Path makers are visionaries and explorers; they are courageous risk takers who are continually pushing out, seeking growth and new horizons. Why? Because they are in touch with their heart center, the place in them that knows there is more to know, more to see . . . essentially, more to be. The word *courage* comes originally from the Latin word *cor*, which means "heart." Path makers are not driven solely by the desire for monetary reward; prosperity in all forms is simply the happy consequence of following their bliss. Instead, they are driven by their passion for and love of life, of the adventure. Another way to state this is that path makers are irresistibly called to the next horizon; they are driven by a vision and the desire to deepen their sense of oneness with the creative principle of expansion that they sense flowing through them. The unintended result is that the principle of abundance is there ahead of them, awaiting their arrival. If we are willing to wake up and pay close attention to those who make things happen (not to be confused with *forcing* things to happen), we'll see we have much to learn from them regarding the relationship between courage, risk taking, passion, and actualizing a life of freedom, purpose, and meaning. As an example, listed here are just a few people who, through courage, conscious intention, and a willingness to take risks, became path makers:

Bill Gates, Steve Jobs, Warren Buffett, Oprah Winfrey, Thomas Edison, Albert Einstein, Leonardo da Vinci, John

Lennon, Rosa Parks, Martin Luther King, Jr., Mahatma Gandhi, Mark Zuckerberg, Mark Cuban, Richard Branson, Thomas Jefferson, Susan B. Anthony, Abraham Lincoln, Harvey Milk, John Glenn, Neil Armstrong, Moses, Jesus, Buddha, Socrates, Mother Teresa, Nelson Mandela, Jackie Robinson, Ellen DeGeneres . . .

Of course this very diverse list could go on indefinitely—and that is my point. There have always been, and always shall be, path makers, those who courageously blaze the trail for others. You might say, "Wait a minute, not everyone on this list was (or is) prosperous," and that too is my point—judge not on appearances. Prosperity is a personal discernment. It is not defined simply by the amount of money you make; it's as much about creating a life that demonstrates the difference you make and the freedom you express in doing so. The common factor among everyone mentioned in the preceding list is courage. If you go back and review the list, you'll see that while each person, in their own way, took immeasurable risks to accomplish their vision, it was their heart (passion) and perseverance that got them there. Some demonstrated it with a great abundance of money; others, by enriching their lives and the lives of countless people with less tangible forms of abundance such as love, reverence, kindness, compassion, generosity, respect, time, and freedom. In either case, each person mentioned in this list demonstrated their willingness to risk, fail, and *risk again*; that is what path makers do.

Defining an Appropriate Risk

Being consciously courageous also requires the wisdom of knowing how to define an appropriate risk. If you take a moment to go back and review the preceding list of people one more time, you'll notice one other common trait, besides courage, among them, and that is wisdom. Somehow each individual was guided to know when, where, and how to venture onto the path and to navigate their way to their destination and their destiny; they learned to listen to that guidance and then follow its lead. The question is, from what source will the wisdom that guides you come? If your guidance comes from any external source, you may have a problem if it is driven by fear. If, on the other hand, you listen to your heart, you'll know what to do, because it is the seat of love; its sole/soul motivation is driven by the desire to do and *be* good. The wisdom and guidance that arises from your heart (not the muscle, but the core of your being—that place within which infinite intelligence lives) will never put you or anyone else in jeopardy or in harm's way. While the human heart— often driven by external input generated by fear, greed, and other human emotions—may spawn harmful actions, the wisdom of your *sacred* heart knows nothing about greed, lack, or limitation because it is connected to the whole, the Universe itself. In other words, the wisdom that guides authentic courage can serve you and others only in beneficent ways that enrich your life and at the same time make the world a better place. With authentic courage, does the risk of loss still exist? Of course it does, and it always will, which is why having the courage to risk, fail, and risk again is a lifetime practice. This is easier to do when you remember the secret to life: you are one with an inexhaustible source.

The question worth pondering is, could you ever see your name being on the list of path makers? Be careful how you respond—because, as you know, the Universe has ears and is listening intently. We would all agree there are millions of people whose names belong on this list—why can't *you* be one of them? Of course the answer is, you can. By now you know the unwritten abundance rule that every master teacher has taught: "Believe you can or believe you can't, because either way, the Universe will help you prove you're right." Do you believe this, not only with your head, but with your heart as well? If so, a new horizon lies just ahead.

THE PRACTICE

Courage and the willingness to risk is always a matter of the lesser giving way to the greater. The question we must be willing to ask ourselves is "What's to be lost and what's to be gained by moving forward, and is it worth the risk?"

"How does one become a butterfly?" she asked pensively. You must want to fly so much that you are willing to give up being a caterpillar.

—**Trina Paulus**

Abundance is a universal principle that is already flowing through every aspect of your life; it can't *not* be operating. Whether that principle is currently being demonstrated as an abundance of more than enough or an abundance of not enough is easy to discern. Just check in with your joy meter, your happiness barometer—your heart—and you'll know in an instant. Can you see any area of your life where you might be able to cooperate with the principle of abundance by courageously taking the risk of letting something go, or by leaving the comfort of a current situation in order to make room for what might be gained in the process? If something is to be gained, something must also be released. What shall it be? If you are not sure, a quick review of rule five, "Be in the Flow," might serve you well at this point.

It is vital to remember that we are not addressing abundance strictly as a demonstration of material things, but as an abundance of whatever creates an enriched, whole life—a life of freedom, purpose, and meaning. In every case it is a matter of energy, in one form or another, flowing freely from the lesser (a belief in limitation), giving way to the greater (a belief in expansion and freedom). It's generally the fear of making a mistake, being rejected, or failing (or sometimes even succeeding) that keeps us from extending ourselves to new growth opportunities; in all three instances, it is the underlying belief in not enough.

Remember, all fear is attached to a concern about loss of something. In the following self-inquiry practice, see if you can discern how courage and risk taking both play an intricate role in activating a flow of abundance in the three most prominent areas of our lives, where we invest a majority of our time, energy, and resources:

- **Relationships:** Are you currently enjoying abundant, healthy, and meaningful relationships? If the answer is no, consider where courage and a willingness to take a risk may support you in activating the principle of abundance in measurable ways. Use the following points as a place to start:

Does the fear of making a mistake, being rejected, or failing (or sometimes, succeeding) keep you from extending yourself to others and creating the relationships you desire? The operative words here are *extend yourself*, and the action that follows is to communicate that which you desire. If you don't risk asking, the answer will always be an automatic no. The Universe is on your side, but it is looking to you for direction. With courage you can leave the burden of rejection on the other party, knowing you did your part. Your role, if the answer is "No thank you, maybe later," is not to take it personally.

Communication does wonderful things; the key is not to assume other people know what you desire. Speak up; be clear, mindful, confident, and articulate; let your needs and desires be known. Remember, it is not always *what* you say that matters, but *how* you say it; the energy behind your words speaks as loudly as the words themselves. Rather than making demands, make requests—without being attached to the result.

Perhaps it's about courageously bringing new energy and intention into your existing relationship(s). Maybe it's about transcending the fear of failure by having the courage to exit a relationship that is not serving or honoring you. Often, because we don't want to make a mistake, the tendency is to cling to what we have out of fear that nothing better will come along. Remember, letting go is a prerequisite for receiving in any form, tangible or intangible. Again, the lesser must give way to the greater. What must you risk letting go of to expand your horizons and experience greater, more abundant relationships?

- **Career:** If you are currently employed, are you finding fulfillment in what you do? If you are not, the question to *courageously* consider is, what is missing from your career? Is it passion and joy; a sense of purpose and meaning; enough income, time, or respect; potential for advancement; training or education; or (fill in the blank)? Is it possible you are clinging to your current position out of fear that there is nothing better out there? The point is, a belief in scarcity—or not enough—can show up in many different guises. If you feel that you are missing any of these things in your job, consider where the fear of making a mistake, asking for what you want, being rejected, or failing (or sometimes, succeeding) may be keeping you from expanding your horizon and having the fulfilling career you desire.

If you are not currently employed but wish to be, the same rules apply. Be willing to examine and challenge any fear of not enough that may be unearthed, including that there are not enough good jobs available. Be courageous. Be willing to explore beyond your comfort zone by extending yourself to every possible work opportunity, remembering that if you don't ask, you can't possibly receive. Again, leave the burden of rejection on the other party. It may even be time to seek a career in an entirely different field; it's never too late to reinvent yourself. If you find the fear of rejection or failure lurking behind career opportunities, remember the secret to life: you are one with an unlimited Universe—the source of all that is. There has never been a shortage of abundance, only a lack of creative, courageous ideas to bring it forth. Once again, the lesser must give way to the greater. What must you risk letting go of in order to expand your horizons and experience the career of your dreams?

- **Spirit, Mind, and Body:** Your entire life comprises the triune unity of spirit, mind, and body. For us to fully live in a human skin, all three are subject to our perceptions of making mistakes, being rejected, and failing. One is no more important than the others because we need all three to exist—and yet we tend to live unaware of this triune unity most the time. You are a spiritual being, a mental (emotional) being, and a physical being—and to create a life worth living requires consciously and courageously integrating all three in your daily life.

When it comes to our spiritual, mental, and physical wellness, most of us don't consider the role that being courageous and taking risks plays until pain and suffering invade our space, making life a less than joyful experience. This is when the "inspiration or desperation" syndrome kicks in. Because we are programmed to seek pleasure and avoid pain, nothing gains our attention quicker than pain, whether physical or emotional; sadly, it seems that change and growth are more easily motivated by desperation than by inspiration.

The problem is, far too often, it is easier to suppress, depress, repress, and deny the messenger named pain than to hear what it has to say. That is often when spirit is forgotten and gets thrown under the proverbial bus by the mind and body—and we mindlessly reach for the instant gratification found in the medicine cabinet, liquor cabinet, or refrigerator, or other means of avoidance. The result is that we end up with bodies that we (along with others) judge and reject and are therefore less than happy living in. Further, our minds end up spending far too much time in the tumultuous turmoil of the past, where regret, frustration, and disappointment reign supreme—or the future, where more of the same awaits us. All of this makes for a perfect breeding ground in our mind for the belief in not enough, where the fear of not just making a mistake but actually *being* a mistake (shame) grows exponentially. It can require great courage to face these facts and do something about them— but you are worth it, yes?

Do you believe that you are entitled to an abundance of *all* good things, including spiritual contentment, enhanced physical health, and emotional well-being? Of course you are, but, as you already know, there is a price to pay. Remembering that the lesser must give way to the greater, what must you risk losing by letting go of the instant gratification that dishonors your spirit and muffles the messenger trying to get your attention? What must you risk losing by courageously embracing what is to be *gained* through delayed gratification and self-discipline? What action must you be willing to initiate; what change is waiting to happen? If you align your spirit with your mind and body and listen intently to your heart, equanimity will follow—and you'll know. Make no mistake about it, living in a manner that mindfully acknowledges and celebrates your spirit, peacefully balances your mind, and respectfully loves and honors your body can be a courageous act.

THE PAYOFF

Whoever said the sky is the limit must not have realized that it's not the sky that limits you; it's your perception of the sky that determines the span of the horizon that calls you to new levels of self-expression and fulfillment.

The health of the eye seems to demand a horizon. We are never tired, so long as we can see far enough.

—Ralph Waldo Emerson

The Universe is perpetually offering you an expanded horizon—a larger piece of the cosmic sky—wherein an abundance of all good things is possible, but, as path makers have always done, you must first have the courage to push the edge of your current belief system, to cut your own path, to take a risk and go beyond the sometimes sacrosanct boundaries (beliefs) you have set for yourself (or have allowed others to set for you). When you cast and embrace an inner vision of the life you wish to live and tenaciously embody that vision, courageously following where it leads, new horizons will appear before you. Dewitt Jones was correct—it's not trespassing to go beyond your own boundaries (current beliefs); the only question is, are you willing to take the risk in doing so? To remain healthy of spirit, mind, and body, you must continue to look up and see new territory and then chart a course that gets you there—even if it means becoming a path maker. To access the principle of abundance, taking action is a prerequisite. It's tempting to stand on the sidelines and watch others "make it happen." It's easy to stare at a new horizon from the rut of complacency and dream about it, and quite another thing to proactively move in its direction. The amazing thing is, once you reach that new land of opportunity, there will be yet another horizon in the distance calling to you, awaiting your arrival. That's what new horizons are all about—they illumine the principle of expansion; they show us there is more to know, more to do . . . and as long as we live in a human skin, there always shall be. You were born into an abundant Universe of infinite potential but you have a role to play; you have to name and claim how abundance translates into the life you call your own. Do you believe in yourself enough to be a path maker, to lead the way? Being courageous is where the journey begins. It's comforting to know the Universe is on your side, yes?

Power Points to Personalize

- **Are you a path maker, path taker, or one who doesn't know or even care that there is a path?** It requires great courage just to look at this question, let alone take responsibility for your answer, but it is essential if you desire to deepen your consciousness and expand your horizons, where abundance in every form awaits you.

- **Risk taking isn't the problem because you already do it every day;** it's the *conscious fear* of risk taking that can immobilize you—especially when facing first-time experiences. All fear is attached to a concern about loss of something. Conscious fear is most easily triggered when the risk of rejection, making a mistake, or failing (or succeeding) lies immediately in front of you. Being courageous doesn't deny fear—it transcends fear.

- **Courage means "of the heart." Path makers are not driven solely by the need to be prosperous;** they are driven by their passion and love of life, by their desire to expand their horizons simply for the adventure of being alive. The happy consequence is that abundance always follows the principle of expansion; by means of the law of cause and effect, the reward that follows path makers is abundance, in whatever the appropriate form may be.

- **Letting go is a prerequisite for receiving in any form;** the lesser must give way to the greater. When it comes to your relationships, your career, and the well-being of your spirit, mind, and body, what must you risk letting go of to expand your horizons and experience greater abundance in its many diverse forms? If you monitor your joy meter, your happiness barometer—your heart—you'll know instantly; while your head may mislead you, your heart is incapable of doing so.

- **It's not trespassing to go beyond your own boundaries (or current beliefs).** The question is, are your mind and heart clear enough to catch the vision of the life that waits for you, lingering just beyond that horizon? You don't require cosmic enlightenment to expand your consciousness or your horizon—just an awareness of your oneness with life and an understanding of how an expanding Universe conspires to enlarge upon itself in and through you every moment of every day.

CHAPTER ELEVEN

Rule 10: Be a Catalyst for Good

*Use the Principle of Abundance to Leave the World
a Better Place Than When You Arrived*

It really boils down to this: that all life is interrelated.
We are all caught in an inescapable network of mutu-
ality, tied in a single garment of destiny. Whatever
affects one directly, affects all indirectly.

—Dr. Martin Luther King, Jr.

THE PREMISE

As our individual abundance consciousness rises, it affirmatively affects the whole of humankind. When we are conscious of our oneness with an abundant Universe and with each other, we are compelled to become change agents for good. This is when our generosity of spirit and our spirit of generosity merge and become a catalyst, guiding our actions, making the world a better place.

Becoming a catalyst for good is the natural culmination of reading *The Art of Abundance*. To assume that the principle of abundance can be used to prosper yourself while at the same time *not* benefit others is errant thinking that violates the universal principle of oneness. Don't think the principle of oneness has anything to do with dishonoring the economy of the free marketplace, where diligence and right effort are personally rewarded, or that it implies we are not individually responsible for creating our own life and shaping our unique destiny; this is not the case because the law of cause and effect is in action. When you understand this law, you will use the principle of abundance consciously, freely, joyfully, as a change agent for good—not because you should but because you can. When you fully embody the principle of abundance you will not be attached to the manner in which others may personally prosper from the good you bring to the world, because you will have transcended the fear of not enough. We could say the generosity of spirit *and* the spirit of generosity will have been so deeply embedded in your heart and mind that you have been set free. Operating freely from a consciousness of oneness with the Universe is liberating; those who do so know there is more than enough to go around, and that awareness becomes cause to the effect of more of the same for them—abundance of every nature.

Remembering your oneness with the Universe is paramount to accessing and using the principle of abundance. At the core of creating a life worth living lies the understanding that we are all on this journey together. From a holistic perspective—a realization of wholeness—the preceding quote by Martin Luther King, Jr., is true whether we know it (or like it) or not. In the web of life, every living being is connected and therefore affected by the actions of others. It can be no other way; what affects the microcosm (the individual) must also affect the macrocosm (humankind), and conversely, what affects the macrocosm must affect the microcosm. As discussed in the eighth Abundance Rule, "Be of Service," this awareness shapes our consciousness in a manner that lifts us from me-thinking to we-thinking. As an example, I recall a conversation I once had with my friend and colleague Dr. Michael Bernard Beckwith, a minister and the founder of the Agape International Spiritual Center. When talking about the success of his good work on the planet, and how his success had positively affected so many people, including other ministers throughout the New Thought movement and beyond, he said, "When we are conscious of our oneness, we know there is no such thing as personal good; when the tide lifts one boat in the harbor, all boats in the harbor rise as well." Can you personalize Beckwith's beautiful sentiment? To be aware of this truth and embrace it as *your* truth makes you a catalyst—a change agent—for good.

What Does It Mean to Be a Catalyst for Good?

If you want to be an agent of change, it starts with you and what you're made of.

—**Michael J. Fox**

While there are several definitions for the word *catalyst*, the common element among them is that a catalyst is something— or someone—that causes increased bonding activity between two or more forces for the purpose of creating something new, something that didn't previously exist. In the realm of the science lab, those change agents (forces) are various chemicals that when commingled create a desired reaction and result. In the realm of humankind, those change agents (forces) are conscious individuals (such as you) whose intention, in every instance, in every type of relationship, is to commingle with others mindfully for a desired purpose that results in a better world for everyone. Irrespective of the relationship—be it with our loved ones, neighbors, work associates, those who serve us in so many wonderful ways, or total strangers—we each have something innately good to bring to the table, to the relationship we have with all humankind. This is when our generosity of spirit (the sharing of the unique essence of who we are as spiritual beings) and our spirit of generosity (the sharing of what we have as earth beings) commingle and ascend, guiding our actions. Accordingly, this is what being a catalyst for good means: bringing your awareness of your oneness with the principle of abundance to bear in a manner that changes the world—*your* world—for the better.

THE PROBLEM

The problem is self-perception; too often, we can't see the gift we innately are. Being a change agent for good in the world doesn't require anything but right intention and a willingness to see yourself and the unique gift you bring as more than good enough and then discerning how best to share that gift with the world.

I want the world to be better because I was here. I want my life, I want my work, my family, I want it to mean something and if you are not making someone else's life better then you are wasting your time.

—Will Smith

Being a catalyst for good in the world may be challenging if we perceive the bucket we bring to the table of life as less than full. Of course the bucket is a metaphor for a lack of consciousness, and the table is the place in the world where we connect with other people, be it on the job, at home, or any other place. Many people hold a vision for their life that is myopic, meaning they are so inwardly focused on their own perceived needs and what's missing in their lives that there is no space in their consciousness for being a catalyst for positive change. They are more focused on what they can *get* from the world than on what they can *bring* to the world. This may be because they feel isolated, alone, and cut off from the world, rather than one with the world. It might also be because they are enmeshed in the belief in not enough—both "there is not enough" and "I am not enough." (How can we bring our gift to the world if we don't value the gift we are?) In either case, this is not pointed out to inflict guilt or shame, but rather to give rise to a new awareness: Is it possible that the two are interrelated—that the feeling of being alone, apart, and separated from the world rather than one with it is what feeds a belief in not enough? In addition, could it be that by getting outside ourselves and our perceived limitations—by courageously extending ourselves to others in some manner that connects us and makes the world a better place—we also then unite with the source of more than enough? Of course, the answer is yes. By intentionally becoming a catalyst for good in the world, we are also simultaneously being drawn closer to the source of our own good. The lingering question that awaits an answer is, "How will you show up as the gift of goodness, the catalyst that changes the world for the better?"

WIIFM

As we evolve consciously we discover that a shift takes place in our goals, agendas, motivations, and intentions. We begin to actually see ourselves and our world differently; our metaphoric myopia self-corrects and the vision of a life worth living comes more clearly into focus, including—rather than excluding—the wholeness of others. At some level, we know we are on a mission to give something special and unique to life rather than merely see how much we can get from it. This is often referred to as the WIIFM principle. The acronym asks a question that, depending on how fully we have developed our awareness of our oneness with the source of our abundance, can be interpreted either of two ways: What's In It *For* Me? or What's In It *From* Me? Understanding that we are all connected in the web of life, as we evolve in an abundance consciousness, we are compelled to ascend from me-thinking to we-thinking; in the process, the perceived separation between us and others narrows. As we know from the fifth Abundance Rule, "Be in the Flow," we need not concern ourselves with what returns to us because the law of reciprocity (circulation) is on the job—what goes around comes around. Depending on what WIIFM means to you, that is either the good news or the other news. If, at the end of your stay on the planet, the world is a better place than it was the day you arrived—because you were here—your mission was a success; you were a catalyst for good, and that is very good news indeed, for everyone.

THE PRINCIPLE

As with initiating any change, the best place to start is the mirror. If you want to change the world for the better, begin by changing yourself for the better; in the process you'll not only discover your purpose, you'll uncover the gift you are— and you'll also see that the ripple effect of you truly matters to the world.

You cannot hope to build a better world without improving the individuals [in it]. To that end each of us must work for his or her own improvement.

—**Marie Curie**

The reason many people fall short of being a catalyst for good is they believe they have nothing of value to offer. Having a low sense of self-worth naturally leads to having no true sense of purpose, which in turn leads to a lack of vision. Do you see your life and what you do with it as purposeful? Do you see the gift you bring as worthy? It's not as difficult as you might first imagine to discover that who you are—and what you do with who you are—affects others, perhaps without your even realizing it. With all that is happening on our planet and between nations, it's easy to perceive our individual selves as insignificant and isolated; in the process, we get lost in what we interpret as the minutiae of our own personal existence. Six degrees of separation is the idea that every human being on the planet is six or fewer steps away (by means of introduction) from any other person. This means the world is smaller than we may imagine and that who we are and what we do with who we are, in no small manner, matters to others.

> The idea that everything is purposeful really changes the way you live. To think that everything that you do has a ripple effect, that every word that you speak, every action that you make affects other people and the planet.
>
> **—Victoria Moran**

I share a personal story with you because it illustrates how this awareness became a reality in my own life. Occasionally I receive kind notes from people who have read my books. Often they share their story of how something they read made a difference in their life. As an author, I am always humbled and honored to receive such communications. Having said this, one day, while zipping through a cache of backed-up emails, I opened one that especially caught my attention. This note was from a gentleman who had just read *The Art of Uncertainty: How to Live in the Mystery of Life and Love It*, and he was telling me how the book had affected him and that he was sharing it with some of his friends. Of course, that brought a smile to my face. He went on to share how grateful he was that the book had been translated into Persian (Farsi) . . . and that is what caught me by surprise. While several of my books have been translated into various foreign languages, I had no idea one had been translated into Persian without going through the traditional process of acquiring foreign language publishing rights. This is because Iran has never been part of the Berne Convention agreement recognizing international copyright laws.

At first, I recoiled a bit with the news because it meant that the book had been published halfway around the world without my consent or awareness. Of course this was Mr. Ego (a.k.a. mini-me) taking it personally. Then, in a heartbeat, a subtle and peaceful voice whispered in my ear, "Yes, but think of the ripple effect. There is wonderful news here— consider the lives that you would have never otherwise touched who will be affected positively because this has happened." That deeper voice never fails to deliver when I am willing to hear it. The moral of this story is, this isn't just about me being a change agent, connecting with people on the other side of the planet in a manner I could never, in a million years, have made happen on my own; it's about you and the fact that we are all ripple makers—which means we can all be change agents for good, making the world a better place, perhaps in small but profoundly meaningful ways to others. Small is the way the ripple effect begins; however, if you can visualize a pond of calm water just after a pebble has been dropped into it, the ripple doesn't remain small. The further the ripple expands, the more the water is affected— and soon, multiple ripples appear, caused by the first one.

Have you ever thought of yourself as a pebble? Metaphorically speaking, on the pond of life, that is exactly what you are when you consider those who are affected by the ripple effect of your thoughts, deeds, and actions. You might even be a rock, turning ripples into waves. Just consider the lives you touch during the span of a day, a year, or a lifetime, perhaps without ever realizing it. If we are all separated by only six degrees or fewer, maybe it's the Universe's way of helping us discover the secret to life—our oneness, our interconnectedness—and the ripple effect is the connective tissue that ties us together.

The point to remember is that you matter far more than you may realize; everything you do has an effect on someone, somewhere, whether you know them or not. I thank my new friend in Iran for sending me an email making me aware of the Persian translation, and the translator for honoring the intent of my words. In the process these people have become pebbles—change agents for good—sending out ripples that continue to touch other lives. The same goes for you as well. It might be a stranger on the other side of town who is affected by a kind and loving word you extended to your neighbor while passing on the sidewalk, who in turn extended an act of kindness to that person. Then again, it could be a friend or stranger on the other side of the planet who is affected via the ripple effect you initiated when you posted an inspiring thought on Twitter, or that special picture or story on Facebook that touched hearts and put a smile on everyone's face, which they then share with others, and so on it goes. Being a catalyst for good, making the world a better place, happens with grace and ease when your intention and purpose are clear. Can you see how the principle of abundance manifests in so many remarkable, demonstrable ways when you are consciously aware that you are the channel through which good, in many forms, flows to the world?

The Question That Awaits an Answer

The question you must ask yourself isn't "Will I make a difference in the world?" The real question is "What kind of difference will it be?" If the ripples you send forth this day are guided by an abundance of loving-kindness, nonjudgment, reverence, compassion, joy, generosity of spirit, and the spirit of generosity, you may be assured you are being a catalyst for good, and that is a high calling. This is what our world needs and you are being called—you are the perfect pebble to make some mighty waves. As always, be not concerned about prospering in whatever way serves you, because abundance follows the ripple effect. As we learned in the second Abundance Rule, "Be Aware You Live in an Expanding Universe," it's simply the principle of expansion doing what it does best—pushing out, creating more than enough from itself.

THE PRACTICE

Just as you can't give what you don't have, you cannot expect others to give, be, or do something you are not willing to give, be, or do. Thinking the right thing is good, and saying the right thing is appropriate, but doing the right thing is what defines you.

If we could change ourselves, the tendencies in the world would also change. As a man changes his own nature, so does the attitude of the world change towards him. We need not wait to see what others do.

—**Mahatma Gandhi**

The moment you picked up this book you enrolled as a change agent for good because I suspect that in your heart you already knew the secret to life; reading *The Art of Abundance: Ten Rules for a Prosperous Life* only clarified, anchored, and affirmed it in your mind. However, as one of my teachers once put it, "Realization without application is hallucination." Unless we take what we have learned and put it to work in our lives, it is all for naught and we stay stuck in a fantasy world, wishing from a distance that things in our lives and on the planet would change for the better. The reality is that change begins with you.

Being a catalyst for good is not a part-time job. As we discovered in the eighth Abundance Rule, "Be of Service," living in the flow of an abundance consciousness encompasses every aspect of your life. From the moment you arise in the morning until the moment you lay your head on the pillow at night, the opportunity to be a catalyst for good, to make the world a better place, lies right before you—at home, at work, and everywhere else. The reason more people are not conscious catalysts for good in the world is that they don't know where to start; after all, changing the world for good sounds like such a monumental task—but you'll soon learn otherwise. To prime the pump, begin where you are, with the smallest of acts, and work your way up. Consider the following suggestions as a place to start:

1. Be mindful that your success in the world can be found in the cracks and crevices of your daily life; you don't have to be a billionaire, a brain surgeon, or a scientist who discovers the cure for a major disease to be a change agent for good. Ralph Waldo Emerson shared in the following quote a beautiful vision of what being successful in life looked like to him. Notice that there is no mention of money, fame, or material gain—only the satisfaction found in making the world a better place by means of the seemingly smallest of acts and deeds.

   "Success: To laugh often and much, to win the respect of intelligent people and the affection of children, to earn the appreciation of honest critics and endure the betrayal of false friends, to appreciate beauty, to find the best in others, to leave the world a bit better, whether by a healthy child, a garden patch, or a redeemed social condition; to know even one life has breathed easier because you have lived. This is to have succeeded!"

Consider Emerson's vision of success the next time you interact with a family member, a coworker, or a stranger. How might you employ some of his suggestions? It's not just what you do in the world, it's how you do it—it's the manner, mindfulness, consciousness, and intention with which you show up. This is a beautiful example of how the principle of abundance encompasses far more than material gain. As an energy conduit, when you mindfully present yourself in the moment as a catalyst for good—irrespective of where you are or what you are doing—the ripple effect of *you* goes before you.

Remember, you have no idea how far into the world the energy of your good intentions may flow, nor what form they may take. This is why Emerson's methodology of making the world a better place in such a variety of seemingly subtle, nonmaterial, selfless ways is so brilliant; in a roundabout way, it has everything to do with the principle of abundance. Because you are established in an abundance consciousness, you have no attachment to the manner in which you disseminate your energy, time, and resources because your intentions are right and good; you know that energy spent must return to you in kind, in unknown, unexpected, and beautiful ways that make the world—and thus *your* world—a better place.

2. One of the characteristics of an individual who under-
   stands that they are a catalyst for good is their ability to
   practice mindfulness. They know that wherever they
   are, whatever they are doing, their opportunity to be a
   change agent lies directly in the moment at hand. It's not
   a matter of one day being in a position to be the one who
   makes the difference—it's a matter of remembering that
   as conscious conductors of energy, we carry within us
   the most powerful tools possible to effect positive change
   in the world: our consciousness, our attitude, and our
   ability to courageously hold ourselves accountable by focusing on what's right and good in life, and sharing that
   perspective with others.

   If you doubt you have the ability to be a "light bearer"
   and a change agent, consider the following as a mindfulness practice. You'll see you have a greater impact on the
   world than you may know.

- Before you walk through the open door of your home
  tonight, pause for a short moment, breathe, and do some
  self-inquiry. Silently ask yourself, "Who is it I bring into
  this home tonight? Is it a conscious person who realizes
  their oneness with life? Will I use the power of my presence, my actions, and the words I speak to lift and love
  those I share this part of my world with?" In so doing,

you are being a catalyst for good. Step through the door and observe the light you bring with you. This is the principle of abundance flowing through you as the generosity of spirit.

• Before you walk through the open door of your workplace, pause for a moment, breathe, and, again, do some self-inquiry. Silently ask yourself, "Who is it I bring into this work environment today? Is it a conscious person who knows they are here to make a difference by bringing their highest and best self to the tasks at hand? Will I freely use my gifts and talents today in a manner that honors this part of my world—my employer, fellow workers, and those I serve in this organization?" When you arrive at a solid yes in consciousness, mindfully step through the door, knowing you are a change agent for good. This is the principle of abundance flowing through you as the spirit of generosity.

• Now that you have the idea, carry the practice with you as you move through the day. Before you get behind the wheel of your car, before you walk through the door of the grocery store, post office, or even the unemployment office, mindfully pause and ask yourself the simple question, "Who is it I bring with me in *this* moment . . . is it the one I know who came here to make this part of my world, in this moment, a better place?" Then breathe, smile, and silently affirm, it is indeed. Notice that the energy you feel in that moment is your essence fully entering into the flow of life . . . and you know what follows, yes? The principle of abundance, of course. This is bringing the wholeness of you to the table of life.

3. As we know from the fifth Abundance Rule, "Be in the Flow," most people spend a large portion of their lives doing some sort of work ("making" a living) by exchanging a certain amount of their precious time and energy for a paycheck (another form of energy). As you evolve in an abundance consciousness and your awareness of your oneness with life deepens, one particular question is bound to arise; when it does, you will have the opportunity to reconcile your beliefs with your actions. That question is, "Does what I do for a living contribute to making the world a better place for everyone?" Does your work allow you to be a catalyst for good in our world, or is it simply a means to an end, a way to survive and pay the bills? In the case of the latter, it is a noble and good thing to work to pay the bills—you are demonstrating abundance at a meaningful and purposeful level. However, the burgeoning change agent within each of us includes a vision that takes us beyond simply paying the bills; it means doing the right thing, adding something good, something life-affirming, to the world in which we live. A few examples might be:

- If you earn a living cleaning houses, don't just go through the routine of cleaning each house; visualize yourself making the world a more beautiful place one house at a time.

- If you are a trash collector, don't just pick up the garbage; see yourself making your community a more sanitary place, one street at a time.

- If you are a dog walker, be the most compassionate and considerate dog walker you can be. Walk the dog with an awareness of your oneness with the animal. Know that you are assisting that dog in staying healthy.

- If you work as a receptionist, remember that you are the first person people entering the office will encounter. Greet each one mindfully with a smile, knowing that your smile may initiate the ripple effect that changes their day.

It's not just what we do to earn a living that matters; it's the consciousness and intention with which we do that which is ours to do. In the tradition of Buddhism, "right livelihood" is practiced as part of the Noble Eightfold Path, and it offers a powerful perspective regarding this issue. The practice of right livelihood takes into consideration the manner in which one earns a living. It is a litmus test of sorts to discern if the work one does serves and honors the wholeness of life.

The Eightfold Path was written thousands of years ago; the

discourse on right livelihood was intended to instruct the people *of that time* how they might earn a living in a manner that alleviated pain and suffering for themselves and others. Some principles and practices are timeless; it's likely that Buddha also realized he was setting an exquisite example—a prototype— of how each one of us can choose to be the one who makes the difference for the many. In his book *What the Buddha Taught*, Walpola Rahula, a Sri Lankan Buddhist monk and scholar, writes:

> Right Livelihood means that one should abstain from making one's living through a profession that brings harm to others, such as trading in arms and lethal weapons, intoxicating drinks or poisons, killing animals, cheating, etc., and should live by a profession which is honorable, blameless and innocent of harm to others.

Of course, only you can interpret the context and degree to which you may choose to incorporate the concept and practice of right livelihood in your life. It's not difficult to discern whether what you do to generate income adds to or takes away from your ability to be one who makes the world a better place. If you discover that the work you are doing doesn't honor your calling to be a catalyst for good, be open to guidance from within and allow yourself to hear what your soul self has to say. You may be surprised by what is revealed—you may discover a more satisfying manner to optimize the gift you are, the gift you bring to the world that only you can deliver.

As you evolve in your abundance consciousness, remembering there is only one of us here, the livelihood you choose to make your own will not only generate prosperity for you, it will also generate ripples of goodness that extend far beyond the span of your stay on the planet—and that is the mark of a true change agent, one who leaves the world a better place than it was when they arrived.

THE PAYOFF

Being a catalyst for good in the world connects you directly to the secret of creating an abundant life: your oneness with the Universe. When you are guided intuitively to do the right thing, the world benefits greatly from your being alive; in turn, you benefit greatly from being alive.

Happiness and personal fulfillment are the natural consequences of doing the right thing.

—Epictetus

As Epictetus observes, happiness and self-fulfillment are always in hot pursuit of the one who does what's right—not just for themselves, but for humankind. But, what does "doing the right thing" mean? It's such an open-ended mandate; is there wiggle-room in interpreting what the "right thing" is that allows us to fudge a bit? Is there a test of some sort that tells us how well we are doing the right thing? Yes; it's called listening to your heart—that intuitive place within you that knows it is connected to the whole. While your head may easily get seduced into thinking fear thoughts that generate a sense of duality and separation from the wholeness of life, resulting in actions that are self-serving—or that fall short of doing the right thing—your heart is incapable of lying to you; it knows the truth. Ask yourself the following questions and listen to how your heart responds:

- How do you feel about your own development and evolution? Have you grown in the recent past, and are you happy?
- Are you more "awake" now than you were a year ago, or even when you first picked up this book?
- Are you making more conscious choices, those that further your development of all that represents an abundant life?

- Are you adding something positive and constructive to the world that makes it a better place for everyone?

These answers are easy enough to discern. Being a catalyst for good brings out the best in you. You are consciously guided in your financial and business affairs to "think up"—to consider the impact of your actions on the whole (including the environment); you act with deep integrity. Similarly, it affects the choices you make and how you conduct yourself with others, whether family, friends, work associates, or even strangers. As a catalyst for good, you are always in the mode of being in the flow of life in a manner that honors your deepest self. As the saying goes, "As within, so without." In the words of author David Hawkins, "To become more conscious is the greatest gift anyone can give to the world; moreover, in a ripple effect, the gift comes back to its source."

It's safe to say that using the principle of abundance to make a difference by leaving the planet a better place than it was when you arrived falls within the job description of being a change agent for good. It is impossible to assist others in creating success and abundance in their lives without also getting some yourself; it's just the way the principle of abundance works—and that is a beautiful thing.

Power Points to Personalize

- **Being a catalyst for good in the world comes naturally to those who have discovered the secret to creating a prosperous life.** They understand that abundance is a universal principle and that it cannot be used to prosper themselves alone. Because there is really only one of us here, you have a role to play in creating an abundant life that makes the world a better place for all.

- **As we evolve in our awareness of our oneness with life we begin to see ourselves and our world differently.** Our myopic vision self-corrects and the WIIFM principle offers us an opportunity to ask a self-defining question: "Am I focusing more on what I can *bring to* the world than what I can *take from* it?" A consciousness of more than enough to go around or not enough to go around determines the answer.

- **There is never a moment when the ripple effect of *you* doesn't make a difference;** the question is, what kind of a difference will it be? As a conscious conduit of energy, you know that your thoughts and actions become cause to an effect that may extend far beyond you and your immediate world. With the principle of expansion at work, you may never know the lives that have been positively affected by the ripple effect of you.

- **The opportunity to be a catalyst for good lies directly before you, 24-7.** Irrespective of where you are or what you are doing in the abundant life you have created, you have the power to be a change agent for good, to make the world, in some way, a better place. The various forms that good may take are as numerous as the stars in the sky— that is the principle of abundance in action.

- **Being a catalyst for good in the world brings out the best in you.** When you leave this planet and return home—back to the oneness from which you came—you shall leave a trail of energy, the essence of who you were while here, and it will be your legacy to future generations. May you leave the "best of you" behind in your wake. May it be a legacy that is overflowing with examples for others to follow, which point the way to the freedom that awaits anyone who is willing to go beyond the great "barrier reef" called the fear of not enough to access, and mindfully use, the universal principle of abundance, which awaits them there.

CHAPTER TWELVE

Conclusion

To be good is to be in harmony with oneself.

—Oscar Wilde

The biggest challenge we often encounter when determining how we would like our lives to be more abundantly fulfilled is that we tend to overcomplicate the process. We buy into the fallacy that to create a prosperous life requires great sacrifice. It does not. The only thing that has to be sacrificed is our belief in scarcity, in not enough. This belief has become the "sacred cow" that many revere and hold sacrosanct because it justifies, explains, or makes acceptable what appears to be missing in their lives.

Clinging to the belief in not enough helps make sense of a world where scarcity, in one form or another, is a commonly agreed-upon reality. With all that is transpiring in our world, this may sound harsh or uncaring, but that is not my intention. My goal is to start a conversation about breaking free from the legend of not enough, and there is only one place to begin that conversation. To this day, the words of my teacher still ring loudly in my ears: "The world doesn't have a prosperity problem . . . it has a consciousness problem!" As mentioned in the third Abundance Rule, "Be Accountable for Your Consciousness," the belief in scarcity has been a legend passed down from one generation to the next for so many years that it has come to be accepted as a fact, as just the way the world works—and few among us seem willing to challenge the legend. The collective consciousness enveloping this planet is a mighty force with which to contend, and as we awaken and evolve in our understanding of our oneness with life, this topic can no longer be conveniently explained away, swept under the rug, or shamefully avoided, as it has been for millennia.

We cannot leave it to our politicians, big businesses, or even the major religions of the world to correct the problem, because some of them (but certainly not all of them) *are* the problem. Why? It's how they remain in control. The belief in scarcity and the perpetuation of that belief is all about power and control, and it always has been; it is a play of energy between those who have it and those who *believe* they don't have it. Can you imagine how the world's balance of power would shift if every human being on the planet knew the secret to life—their oneness with their source—and claimed the freedom to call back their energy, to take back the power they have unknowingly given away, by embracing and practicing the core concepts found in the ten Abundance Rules?

Challenging and changing this massive belief in not enough has to begin somewhere, sometime, with someone. Why not here? Why not now? Why not you? Why not me? *Why not us?* Why must the legend of not enough continue to trickle downstream for another thousand years? When even one of us can scale the invisible wall of fear that keeps millions of people trapped inside their own personalized version of not enough, by example, we shall be introducing something new into the collective consciousness, something life-changing, the freedom for which every human being longs: to create a life worth living.

> *The Journey Doesn't End with Changing Your Belief in Not Enough; That Is Where It Begins*
>
> Thought is the creative power, or the impelling force which causes the creative power to act; thinking in a Certain Way will bring riches [abundance in many forms] to you, but you must not rely upon thought alone, paying no attention to personal action. That is the rock upon which many otherwise scientific metaphysical thinkers meet shipwreck— the failure to connect thought with personal action.
>
> **—Wallace D. Wattles**

If you recall, in chapter one, in the parable of the fish in the lagoon, upon discovering the secret to life—her oneness with the Great Infinite Ocean, her source—Angel set out from the lagoon a second time, this time to accomplish part two of her assignment. She was being called to action. Angel understood that simply knowing the secret to life was insufficient; she knew that all she had learned would be of no value unless she was able to use her newfound awareness of abundance in a manner that gave her life meaning and fulfillment. In other words, discovering any universal principle—especially the principle of abundance—is useless unless we have the vision and willingness to explore it, to take action to implement the principle, and to *use* it consciously.

The ten Abundance Rules presented in this book are not breaking news; the principles and laws discussed herein are as ancient as the Universe itself and have been floating around the ether in one form or another for thousands of years. The question that demands an answer is, what is it that enables some people to harness and use these laws and principles in a manner that changes their lives, and other people, not so much? Benjamin Franklin gave us the answer very succinctly: "Well done is better than well said." Mark Twain essentially said the same thing, using his own pithy wit to make the point: "Actions speak louder than words, but not nearly as often."

It has been my goal, through the filter of my own consciousness, to present the ten Abundance Rules in a format that engages your mind and heart, ignites a fire in your belly, and puts wheels on your dream. This is where the proverbial rubber meets the road—your call to action. As Wallace Wattles implies in the opening quote, thinking positive, prosperous thoughts alone, without taking the necessary action to implement those thoughts, is a waste of one's time. This moment in time is where your redefining moment awaits your recognition and acceptance. My sole intention in writing *The Art of Abundance: Ten Rules for a Prosperous Life* was to offer a plan, a simple road map that would ultimately bring you back to where your journey began the day you were born: your oneness with life. You already are one with your source of abundance—but you must be willing to venture outside your current comfort zone and use the ten Abundance Rules to guide you and lift you to a new perspective of life through your active implementation of the principles and practices found herein.

1. Be One with Life
2. Be Aware You Live in an Expanding Universe
3. Be Accountable for Your Consciousness
4. Be Focused
5. Be in the Flow

6. Be Passionate

7. Be Blessed

8. Be of Service

9. Be Courageous

10. Be a Catalyst for Good

It has been an honor to have you as my traveling companion on this exploration of a different, perhaps new approach to what living a prosperous life of abundance means. Perhaps one day we shall meet again while on our grand adventure beyond the lagoon.

Peace, *Dennis*

What lies behind us and what lies before us are tiny matters compared to what lies within us.

—Ralph Waldo Emerson

RECOMMENDED READING

Beckwith, Michael Bernard. *Life Visioning*. New York: Sounds True, 2013.

Beckwith, Michael Bernard. *Spiritual Liberation*. New York: Atria Books, 2009.

Breathnach, Sarah Ban. *Simple Abundance*. New York: Grand Central Publishing, 2009.

Butterworth, Eric. *Spiritual Economics*. Unity Village, MO: Unity School of Christianity, 1983.

Campbell, Joseph. *The Power of Myth*. New York: Anchor, 1991.

Chopra, Deepak. *The Seven Spiritual Laws of Success*. New York: Amber-Allen, 1994.

Chopra, Deepak, & Kafatos, Menas. *You Are the Universe*. New York: Harmony Books, 2017.

Covey, Stephen. *The 7 Habits of Highly Effective People*. New York: Simon & Schuster, 2013.

De Mello, Anthony. *Awareness*. New York: Doubleday, 1990.

Dyer, Wayne. *Change Your Thoughts—Change Your Life*. New York: Hay House, 2009.

Dyer, Wayne. *The Power of Intention*. New York: Hay House, 2005.

Elgin, Duane. *The Living Universe*. San Francisco: Berrett-Koehler, 2009.

Emerson, Ralph Waldo. *Essays*. New York: CreateSpace Independent Publishing, 2016.

Ferrucci, Piero. *The Power of Kindness*. New York: TarcherPerigee, 2006.

Hanh, Thich Nhat. *The Heart of the Buddha's Teaching*. New York: Broadway Books, 1998.

Hill, Napoleon. *Think and Grow Rich*. New York: TarcherPerigee, 2005.

Holmes, Ernest. *The Science of Mind*. New York: G. P. Putnam's Sons, 1938.

Holmes, Ernest. *This Thing Called You*. New York: TarcherPerigee, 2004.

Jones, Dennis Merritt. *The Art of Being: 101 Ways to Practice Purpose in Your Life*. New York: TarcherPerigee, 2008.

Jones, Dennis Merritt. *The Art of Uncertainty: How to Live in the Mystery of Life and Love It*. New York: TarcherPerigee, 2011.

Jones, Dennis Merritt. *Your (Re)Defining Moments: Becoming Who You Were Born to Be*. New York: TarcherPerigee, 2014.

Kabat-Zinn, Jon. *Wherever You Go, There You Are*. New York: Hyperion, 1994.

Moran, Victoria. *Living a Charmed Life: Your Guide to Finding Magic in Every Moment of Every Day*. New York: HarperOne, 2010.

Rahula, Walpola. *What the Buddha Taught*, rev. ed. New York: Grove Press, 1974.

Tolle, Eckhart. *A New Earth*. New York: Penguin, 2008.

Wattles, Wallace D. *The Science of Getting Rich*. New York: CreateSpace Independent Publishing, 2013.

Williamson, Marianne. *The Gift of Change*. San Francisco: HarperSanFrancisco, 2006.

Zukav, Gary. *The Seat of the Soul*. New York: Fireside, 1989.

ABOUT THE AUTHOR

Dennis Merritt Jones has been involved in the human potential movement and the field of spirituality as a teacher, mentor, and speaker for more than thirty years. He founded the Center for Spiritual Living in Simi Valley, California, and led it for many years. Jones is the author of *Your (Re)Defining Moments*, *The Art of Uncertainty*, and *The Art of Being*. His books have been recipients of Nautilus Awards. He is also a columnist for *The Huffington Post* and *Science of Mind* magazine.

ALSO BY DENNIS MERRITT JONES

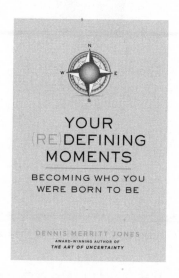

YOUR
(RE)DEFINING
MOMENTS

BECOMING WHO YOU
WERE BORN TO BE

DENNIS MERRITT JONES
AWARD-WINNING AUTHOR OF
THE ART OF UNCERTAINTY

"Dennis Merritt Jones beautifully shows us how every moment provides each individual an opportunity to respond with love instead of react in fear, to choose consciously and constructively instead of unconsciously and destructively—in other words, to create authentic power."

—**Gary Zukav, author** *The Seat of the Soul*

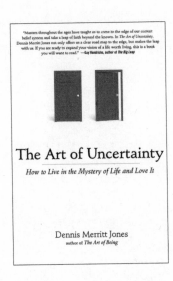

The Art of Uncertainty

How to Live in the Mystery of Life and Love It

Dennis Merritt Jones
author of *The Art of Being*

"Masters throughout the ages have taught us to come to the edge of our current belief system and take a leap of faith beyond the known. . . . If you are ready to expand your vision of a life worth living this is a book you will want to read."

—**Gay Hendricks, author of *The Big Leap***

"Every art requires a great deal of practice to develop. *The Art of Being* provides hundreds of mindfulness exercises that invite you to experiment with your life and shape it with your own creativity."
—Gary Zukav, author of *The Seat of the Soul* and *Soul to Soul*

The Art | of Being

101 Ways to Practice Purpose in Your Life

Dennis Merritt Jones

FOREWORD BY MICHAEL BERNARD BECKWITH

"May this book be your special friend, an introduction to Power and Presence . . . the essence inviting you to be you."

—**Rev. Dr. Michael Beckwith,**
Agape International Spiritual Center